The Gift of
Prophetic
Preaching

The Gift of Prophetic Preaching

A Charismatic Approach

Michael Eaton

New Wine Press

New Wine Ministries
PO Box 17
Chichester
West Sussex
United Kingdom
PO19 2AW

ISBN 978–1–905991–14–3

Typeset by CRB Associates, Reepham, Norfolk
Cover design by CCD, www.ccdgroup.co.uk
Printed in Malta

By the same author

In the Preaching Through the Bible series:

Genesis (3 books), *Exodus* (2 books), *Joshua to 2 Kings* (6 books),
Ezra, Nehemiah, Esther, Joel & Amos, Mark & Luke (3 books),
1 Corinthians (2 books), *Galatians, Ephesians, Colossians,*
1–2 Thessalonians, 2 Timothy, James, 1–2 Peter (2 books).

Other biblical expositions:

Applying God's Law (Exodus 19–24) – Paternoster
Ecclesiastes (Tyndale Commentary) – IVP
Hosea (Focus on the Bible) – Christian Focus
The Way That Leads to Life (Sermon on the Mount) – Christian Focus
Return to Glory (Romans 3:21–4:25) – Paternoster
Living Under Grace (Romans 6–7) – Paternoster
Walk in the Spirit (Galatians 5–6)
Jesus God's Last Word (Hebrews 1:1–2:3) – India
Jesus Cares (Hebrews 2:4–3:11) – India
Entering into Rest (Hebrews 3:12–4:13) – India
1, 2, 3 John (Focus on the Bible) – Christian Focus

In the "theology" series:

Experiencing God – Paternoster
The Story of Jesus – New Wine
Living a Godly Life – Paternoster
Know the Bible – Hodder & Stoughton
The Power of Prophetic Preaching – South Africa
Enjoying God's Worldwide Church – Paternoster
Israel, The Christian and the Hope of Worldwide Revival –
    Sovereign World

Others:

Baptism with the Spirit – IVP
A Theology of Encouragement – Paternoster

Contents

Abbreviations

ASV	American Standard Version
AV	Authorised Version
ESV	English Standard Version
GNB	Good News Bible
JB	Jerusalem Bible
KJV	King James Version
LW	Luther's Works
MT	Masoretic Text
MTP	Metropolitan Tabernacle Pulpit
NAB	New American Bible
NASB	New American Standard Bible.
NCB	The Holy Bible, New Century Version
NEB	New English Bible
NICNT	New International Commentary on the New Testament
NICOT	New International Commentary on the Old Testament
NIV	New International Version
NKJV	New King James Version
NLB	Holy Bible: New Living Translation
NLT	New Living Translation
NPNF, 1	Nicene and Post-Nicene Fathers, series 1
NPNF, 2	Nicene and Post-Nicene Fathers, series 2
NRSV	New Revised Standard Version
PNTC	Pillar New Testament Commentaries
PTTB	Preaching Through the Bible (Sovereign World)
REB	Revised English Bible
RV	English Revised Version
TOTC	Tyndale Old Testament Commentaries

Preface

This book is another one of my series of books on Christian teaching that I have been preaching and writing in recent years. I began with *Living a Godly Life* and *Enjoying the Worldwide Church*. All of these books are summaries of what I have been preaching. I regard "preaching" itself as a theological topic! It comes into my "systematic theology" as part of the Doctrine of Revelation. I have also come to believe one should preach about preaching! Every chapter here is a summary of one, two or several messages that I have preached.

I have no interest in Christian teaching unless it changes the lives of ordinary people. My theology is preached theology. In the original preaching there were more illustrations and local digressions than you have here, and some stories about preaching, but local applications have been omitted from these pages. Preachers have to do their own local application of the message as they go along, without necessarily putting everything they say into the printed versions. I do not include here remarks that I make in my preaching that refer to events that happened on the streets of Nairobi or that were mentioned in yesterday's newspaper or what is showing in the local cinema. I remember how one evening (8th June, 1998) I was referring to the film, *Titanic*, where someone says, "Not even God can destroy this ship." It was showing over the road in Nairobi's Twentieth Century Cinema during the time I was preaching on the doctrine of God. At that time Nairobi City Hall had a bigger congregation than Nairobi's Twentieth Century Cinema, but the cinema had some big congregations during that time as well! So I could not resist including a passing exposition of the remark in Titanic. I remembered my mentor and one-time pastor, Dr Martyn Lloyd-Jones, used to refer to the sinking of the Titanic[1] which took place when he was a twelve-year-old boy. It obviously made an impression on him.

I am restating Christian doctrine in a simple way for Christians interested in the teaching of God's Word. The whole list of my systematic theology at present looks as follows, some of it in the form of unpublished notes distributed within Chrisco Fellowship of Churches, Nairobi.

Introduction
   The Whole Counsel of God (Chrisco)
Experiencing God
   Experiencing God (Paternoster)
   The Beauty of the Lord (Chrisco)
   My Strength and Song (Chrisco)
Honouring God's Creation
Understanding Yourself
Glorifying Jesus Christ
   The Jesus of the Gospels (New Wine)
Appreciating Salvation
Receiving the Holy Spirit
Living a Godly Life
   Living a Godly Life (Paternoster)
   Applying God's Law (Paternoster)
   The Way That Leads to Life: the Sermon on the Mount
      (Christian Focus)
Listening to God
   Know the Bible (Hodder & Stoughton)
   The Power of Prophetic Preaching
      (ASL, South Africa)
Enjoying God's Church
   Enjoying God's Worldwide Church
Preparing for the Future
   The Christian, Israel and the Hope of Worldwide Revival

It invariably takes more than one little book for me to cover the topic. *Enjoying God's Church* added the word "Worldwide" and covered only half of what I wanted to say. There is more to come. "Experiencing God" has now become three books. Although I have the total series in my mind, I try to make each book complete in itself.

If I were looking totally to my own inclinations I would like to write the whole series in logical order, but I have felt that I ought to produce first the ones that I think are more urgently needed in the varying situations I find myself in when I preach in different parts of the world.

Although I try to write in a simple, down-to-earth manner, I emphasize that this is a book of Christian doctrine. It does not have many stories or illustrations and no passing expositions of *Titanic*!

As I have mentioned before, all Bible translations are my own, but as a teenager I grew up with the Revised Standard Verson (RSV) which I still love, and anything Lloyd-Jones preached on got itself printed in my head in the old Authorised Version (AV) of 1611. No doubt these facts affect my translations. When I am preaching I am often translating the original text as I am speaking, but I also keep three translations close at hand: the New International Version (NIV), the New American Standard Version (NASB) and the English Standard Version (ESV). In preaching I tend nowadays to use both my own translations plus whatever is the translation the congregation tends to use the most.

I hope one day to expand my brief introductory manuscript, presently known only to Chrisco Fellowship of Churches, perhaps under the title *How to Learn Christian Doctrine*.

The first draft of this book was written while I was sharing much of this material in Germany in November 2005. It is not logically the **first** of my expositions of the Doctrine of Revelation and I might well expand parts of it at another time. I was in a hurry to get to the topic of "prophetic preaching"! Other places that have heard bits and pieces of this material include Pietermaritzburg and Cape Town in South Africa. My own much-loved people in Data Centra,

Kenyatta Avenue, heard an even earlier version (*Reaching the World with the Word*) of this material, plus some more not included here.

I owe a debt of gratitude to those who were my hosts on these various occasions – my daughter and her family, the Gyslings of Basel; and the Plettenberg family of Ennepetal. *Asante sana!* And to my Saviour, Father, Son and Holy Spirit – "I will give to the Lord the thanks due to his righteousness, and I will sing praise to the name of the Lord, the Most High."

Michael Eaton
Nairobi

Notes

1. See the mention of the *Titanic* (the boat not the film!) in D.M. Lloyd-Jones, *Old Testament Evangelistic Sermons* (Banner of Truth, 1995), p. 66.

I. Defining the Prophetic

The Greatest Need of the World

I believe one of the greatest needs of our world is what I would call "prophetic preaching". But Paul did mention love first! That is an even greater need. The apostle Paul said: *"Follow after love, and eagerly desire the spiritual gifts, especially that you may prophesy"* (14:1). Prophecy is speaking for God with special enablement such that one's words are God-given. In prophesying God "puts words in the mouth". It is clear in the Bible that there are various levels and various kinds of prophecy, and I am concerned with one of them – prophetic preaching. In 1 Corinthians 14:1–5, Paul is discussing two spiritual gifts that were clearly causing some difficulties in Corinth. He asks the Corinthians to seek both the gifts of the Spirit and the life of love.

We have to begin with love

We have to put love first. *"Follow after love . . . "* We have to be godly men and women, and if you want to know what godliness is, it is love. Do you follow after love? It takes some of us a long time to take this seriously. I am embarrassed to think how long it was before I began to take love seriously – but we have to do it. We have to work out graciousness towards other people. I am still learning how to do it and am embarrassed by my failures! But it is the number one demand upon our lives. It is giving what the other person truly needs – not what they want, not what they think they need, but what they really need. Love is being totally un-defensive about ourselves. The biggest problem in all our lives is "self", but we have to conquer self and become people of love. Love is greater than the greatest of gifts. If I am a great preacher, as good as Billy Graham, as great an orator as Martyn Lloyd-Jones, as knowledge-able as John Calvin, as gifted a reformer as Luther, and can speak like an angel, but have not love, I have become only a noisy gong or a clanging symbol. God asks love of us, much more than He asks us to become great preachers. If I am the greatest expositor, if I have an understanding of mysteries, if I have faith so as to remove mountains – and moving a congregation towards serving God is as great as moving a mountain! – but do not have love, I am nothing (13:2). Love is slowness to act when we are feeling angry. Love slows us down when we are inclined to act hastily. Hate jumps into situations too quickly. Love is self-restraining. Love is nice to enemies. Christ is the greatest example to us. He constantly faced enmity and slander, but was slow to do anything about it.

Positively, love is kind. It takes trouble to be a means of blessing to the other person. Just as God makes His sun to shine upon the evil and the good, so the kindly person has a warm heart towards all people everywhere. Kindliness is prayerful about others. It prays for enemies. Paul asks us to deliberately estimate love above enthusiasm for charismatic life, above doctrine and intellectual skills, above great practical endeavours. He asks us to think of ourselves as spiritual weaklings and nonentities unless we are conscious that God is leading us into the pathways of love. We might gather a lot of attention to ourselves, as does a noisy gong or a clanging symbol. People might be impressed by our many skills and gifts. We may gain a reputation for sacrifice and dedication. But only love will bring us the approval of God. Only to people of love will Jesus say, "Well done!" God is love. We are only godly men and women if we become like Him in His loving patience and loving kindliness. The challenge before us is a great one.

Love is free from jealousy. There is a spirit of rivalry deep in the nature of all of us. Love is free from boastfulness, free from scornfulness, free from self-centredness, free from resentment. It takes little notice when it is ill-treated. This is what the love of Jesus is. In Jesus God does not reckon our sins against us (2 Corinthians 5:19). Love is like this. We remember Jesus' prayer that His enemies would be forgiven (Luke 23:34). *"Love always endures, always believes, always hopes, always perseveres"* (13:7). This description tells us how love faces adversity from other people. It always endures. It bears up under the distress of hate or opposition or painful failure in another person. It always trusts. Love is the opposite of having a sceptical spirit. It never loses faith in the possibility that God will change the situation. Love always hopes. It is optimistic about the other person, without being gullible. Even if the situation is terrible now, love hopes for better things in the future. It maintains the hope that God will change the situation. It loves the other person enough to hope that change is coming. Love always perseveres. It does not easily give up. 1 Corinthians 13:8a is the conclusion at this point, as well as being the starting point of 13:8–13. *"Love never fails."* This partly means that love never gives up. Even when rebuffed and refused, it goes on. Even when it finds no response in the other person it does not fall to the ground.

Love is being like Jesus. 1 Corinthians 13 could easily be a description of Jesus. Love is eternal, it will never end. Anything that does the will of God abides for ever and love certainly is doing the will of God. *"Now at this time faith, hope, love, these three things, are continuing. But the greatest of these is love"* (13:13b). It is no good wanting to be a prophetic preacher if we are not people of love. *"Anyone who prophesies speaks to people for their strengthening and encouragements and comfort"* (14:3). Prophecy and preaching are not **exactly** identical but they overlap. Like any kind of prophecy, preaching has to be comprehensible and helpful to people! So it has to come out of a heart of love – for God and for His people.

Some big topics

Prophetic preaching is a big topic, an overwhelming topic. Anyone who thinks he can write about prophetic preaching and is not overwhelmed at the audacity of what he is daring to do does not know what preaching is. Dr Martyn Lloyd-Jones, who I suppose was the greatest preacher in the English language in the twentieth century, said, "I have a feeling that I have only really preached twice in my life, and on both occasions I was dreaming."[1] Prophetic preaching is something miraculous. It is not any old kind of public speaking. It is not what is **usually** called "preaching" – walking into a pulpit or on to a platform and saying a few things at church on Sunday morning. A lot of that can hardly be called prophetic preaching! I will do my best to share what I have to say about prophetic preaching, but it is a scary thing to try to do. Who is worthy? *"Who is sufficient for these things"* (2:16b) said Paul. The task of prophetic preaching is such a great one. We are not to be *". . . peddlers of God's word like so many, but in Christ we are to speak as persons of sincerity, as persons sent from God and people standing in his presence"* (2:17). There were many people around in Corinth who were "peddlers" – people who teach a religious message because of the money they get for doing so. But who is sufficient for these things? The answer is: the person who is sent by God with a God-given message of salvation in the Lord Jesus Christ is sufficient, is adequate! But the greatness of the task is almost overwhelming. We are adequate when we are a pen in the hands of the Lord Jesus Christ! *"It is not that we are confident in ourselves to claim that anything is coming from us, but our adequacy comes from God"* (3:5). God creates "ministers" of the New Covenant. Only a fool rushes in to talk about preaching without knowing what he is doing.

The subject of prophetic preaching is part of the total doctrine of "Revelation, Inspiration and Authority" – the teaching of the Bible that has to do with how God speaks to us, how we hear His voice, and how we share what He says with the wider world. It would sub-divide into about seven sections: how God speaks **generally**, how God speaks about **salvation**, how God speaks **through people** (Moses, the prophets, wise men, apostles – supremely how God speaks through our Lord Jesus Christ). Then we would have to come to the doctrine of **Scripture**, the written form of the Word of

God. The Bible has teaching about itself! This would lead us on to the subject of **hermeneutics** – which is the technical term for the study of "principles of interpretation and application". Even when we believe the Bible is the inspired Word of God we still have to face the fact that people sometimes use the Bible in peculiar ways and we should learn how to take it in a straightforward manner without misusing it. It is a topic worth thinking about. Sixth in my list is the question of **authority**. What is the authority in the Church – if any? Of course nowadays people don't like "authority" at all! But the opposite of authority is chaos; when "there was no king . . . all the people did just as they pleased" – but the results were disastrous.

This all leads us to the subject of **prophetic preaching**, which is where I want to begin. For the next question – if we proceed in an orderly manner – is how is this amazing gospel of the Lord Jesus Christ to be communicated to the world? One answer is: by the witness of God's people. They are to know us by our love. We are a chosen people, a royal priesthood, a holy nation, a people belonging to God. We are meant to declare the praises of the one who called us out of darkness into His wonderful light. We are to live such good lives that men and women glorify God on the day He visits us. A sobering and challenging thought! But another answer is: **God gives the gift of prophetic preaching to His people**.

I do not regard myself as an expert on preaching! Who does? Who can? Even the greatest preachers have never thought of themselves as great preachers! "It is almost always the fact that my speech displeases myself", said the great Augustine of Hippo. "My capacities of expression prove inferior to my inner apprehensions . . . I grieve over the inability which my tongue has betrayed in answering to my heart . . . This arises mainly from the circumstance that the intellectual apprehension diffuses itself through the mind with something like a rapid flash, whereas the utterance is slow, and occupies time . . ." I know what he means! "It is a common occurrence with us that, in the ardent desire to effect what is of profit to our hearer, our aim is to express ourselves to him exactly as our intellectual apprehension is at the time, when, in the very effort, we are failing in the ability to speak; and then, because this does not succeed with us, we are vexed, and we pine in weariness as if we were applying ourselves to vain labours..." Yes, I know the feeling! Still Augustine did not give up. "I gather that they derive some profit from it," he said about his sermons. "So far as the Christian orator succeeds, he will succeed more by piety in prayer than by gifts of oratory," he said. Augustine knew that good preaching is simply the inspiration of the Holy Spirit. "When the hour for speech arrives, let him reflect upon that saying of our Lord's as better suited to the wants of a pious mind: 'Take no thought how or what you shall speak; for it shall be given you in that same hour what you will speak. For it is not you that speak, but the Spirit of your Father who speaks in you.' The Holy Spirit, then, speaks thus in those who for Christ's sake are delivered to the persecutors; why not also in those who deliver Christ's message to those who are willing to learn?"[2]

I identify with Augustine! But, despite my inadequacies, there is one reason why I have felt compelled to put these thoughts of mine into print, and that is that the subject of prophetic preaching should be part of our total preached theology. If we are proclaiming "the whole counsel of God" – which is my calling in life – we have no choice but to face this part of the whole counsel of God. If I am to talk about "declaring all that God wants for you" (NIV), "announcing to you the whole purpose of God" (GNB), telling you "everything God wants you to know" (NCB) – then this must be part of my agenda! Prophetic preaching is itself a theological topic which must come into our systematic theology as part of the Doctrine of Revelation. I have come to believe one should preach about preaching!

So the remainder of what we might have to say divides itself into numerous sub-topics. Let me list some of them, but hasten to add: there is a lot in connection with prophetic preaching where I do not feel qualified to speak or write anything! But here is my list. **First,** we always have to keep in mind what we mean by prophetic preaching.

Second, we have to ask the question, Is it possible to prepare for prophetic preaching? My answer is: the prophetic **preacher** has to have some kind of preparation, both in technical knowledge and in the art of expository meditation. Connected with this is the lifestyle of this kind of preacher. How does he spend his time? What is his daily routine? What kind of Bible study and praying does he do? How much time does he give to it? And so on. **Thirdly**, we might want to consider the call of God to prophetic preaching. A **fourth** topic might be to ask the question: is it possible to train a person in the ministry of prophetic preaching. Then, **fifthly**, there are questions concerning the practicalities of delivering the message. Should we ever try to preach a series of prophetic messages from God, and if so how do we go about it? Some of these questions I have tackled elsewhere.[3] The **sixth** and the greatest of them is: how can we find the power of the Spirit to preach as we ought?

Here my theme is the gift of prophetic preaching, and we consider four of these topics, the definition of prophetic preaching, the technical knowledge that is needed, the art of expository meditation, and – more important than anything – the power that is needed.

The greatest need of the world is to be loved. God has already loved the world. Now we have to love the world too, and part of what that means is that we have to bring to the world the gospel-message of Jesus. Some of us are called to do it with the gift of prophetic preaching. My concern is with the practicalities of doing it!

Notes

1. D.M. Lloyd-Jones, "What is Preaching?", in *Knowing the Times* (Banner of Truth, 1989), p. 263.
2. Augustine, *On the Catechising of the Uninstructed*, ch. 2; Augustine, *Christian Doctrine*, book 4, ch. 15. Various editions.
3. See M.A. Eaton, "God-Centred Preaching", "Preaching Through a Book", "Expository Preaching", in G. Haslam (ed.), *Preach the Word* (Sovereign World, 2006), pp. 101–111, 125–135, 161–170; *The Power of Prophetic Preaching* (ASL, South Africa).

Defining "the Prophetic"

The term I am using in these chapters is "prophetic preaching". I have to use such a phrase because nowadays people have all sorts of procedures and techniques in mind when they use the word "preaching" – procedures and techniques in which I have no interest at all! Personally I do not use the word "preaching" to include the use of "Christian cinema" or reciting poems or performance of theatrical drama in the Sunday morning Christian meeting. I do not want to get into the rights and wrongs of such procedures. I cannot condemn them but they are not my topmost priority, and if those things are "preaching" I shall have to find another term to describe more precisely what I wish to write about. "Prophetic preaching" is the right term, I believe.

But what do we mean – or ought we to mean – when we use the Bible term "prophecy" or the adjective that comes from it, "prophetic"? I define prophecy as follows: *it is speaking for God with words given by God*. Perhaps the greatest need of the Church is prophetic expository Bible preaching. I stress each word: **prophetic – Bible – expository – preaching**. But what do we mean by "prophetic"?

The definition comes from Deuteronomy 18:18. "I will raise up for them a prophet . . . I will put my words in his mouth, and he shall speak to them all that I command him." This gives us a biblically required definition of a prophet. As much as possible we should try to use Bible words in the manner in which they were used

originally. "I appointed you a prophet," said God to Jeremiah
(Jeremiah 1:5). Then comes the explanation of what prophecy
involves. "I have put my words in your mouth" (Jeremiah 1:9).
Prophecy is speaking for God with words given by God. One
respected Greek dictionary defines *prophēteia* as "inspired utterance" and *prophēteuō* as to "speak inspired utterances".[1]

Levels of prophecy: Inspired Scripture

It seems that there are levels of prophecy and different types of
prophecy. Let us consider some of them beginning with the
prophetic inspiration of Scripture. When we read of Old Testament prophets it is obvious that their inspiration was operating at a
very high level. When the prophets of the Old Testament wrote and
spoke they dared to start their messages with words like, "This is
what the LORD says . . ." or "This is an oracle of the LORD . . ." They
regarded Yahweh Himself as the speaker of what they were saying.
What they say is what God says. They have a God-given, word-
by-word, inspiration. Because they are verbally inspired their
teaching is without error. Their preaching included both prediction
(foretelling the future) and words of warning and exhortation
(forth-telling) without special prediction. When they did make
predictions their statements concerning the future had to do with
the coming of God's kingdom and His King, after purifying
judgments. The prophets were primarily reformers preaching
repentance and calling God's people to the faithfulness to the
worship of Yahweh. At times their prophecies became authoritative
Scripture.

Does this kind of prophecy exist today? No. There is little or
nothing that is verbally inspired in this manner and announces any
kind of new doctrines. I would have to be critical and unfavourable
towards anyone who made such claims. Certainly no one can write
a book that can be put on a level with the Bible. No one can come
up with a new doctrine, a new interpretation of salvation-history
and then claim verbal inspiration for his statements about it.

Revelation-inspiration **at the biblical level** has ceased, at least until the Second Coming of Jesus (when there will no doubt be some new things to learn!). Prophecy still exists – I have no doubt of that – but it exists at a lower level than what we have in inspired Scripture.

So the most important and reliable "prophetic" message is the teaching of Scripture. Some people use the word "prophetic" as a **contrast** to the Bible. "We need less Bible and more of the prophetic," they say. When they talk about "the prophetic" they mean something **different** from the Bible. But is this right? Do we not regard the Bible as prophetic at all!? When Romans 16:26 talks about "prophetic writings" it refers to Old Testament Scripture. The Bible came as the result of God-given revelations. It is the highest form – and a written form – of the prophetic. One book of the New Testament, Revelation, claims to be prophecy, received directly from God (Revelation 1:1–3; 22:12–20). So how can any Christian **contrast** Scripture and prophecy? The Bible is "inscripturated" prophecy. When it comes to us in the power of the Holy Spirit it **is** (not was) God's Word. This is surely our greatest need – that God should speak to us from His written Word when it comes to us in a preached and applied form in the power of the Holy Spirit. Notice the present tense in Hebrews 1:6–8; 3:7; 5:6; 8:8. God says (not said), "Let all God's angels worship him." Of the Son He says (not said), "Your throne, O God, is forever and ever." As the Holy Spirit says (not said), "Today, if you hear his voice . . ." In each case Hebrews is quoting the Old Testament. The Bible is not what God "said". By the Holy Spirit it becomes what God "says". The Bible when used by God becomes "prophetic word" once again just as it was "prophetic word" in its origins.

Levels of prophecy: Inspiration without Revelation?

Could there perhaps be **verbal inspiration without new revelation**? Some forms of preaching and poetry-writing seem to come close to being verbally inspired, but personally I would be wary about attributing verbal infallibility to any sermon or composition that I have ever come across outside of Scripture. On the other hand I am conscious that my pastor and mentor, Dr Martyn Lloyd-Jones of Westminster Chapel, sometimes used language which implied such "inspiration" might still exist, but without the revelation of any new doctrines. He thought some of the great hymn writers writing in times of revival had "inspiration but not revelation". Their words were being given them – thought Lloyd-Jones – but they were not revealing any new doctrine. "The Holy Spirit enabled these men who wrote the Scriptures to write this inspired, authoritative, inerrant Word of God, but, thank God, the same Spirit can enable a man to compose a hymn, or a song." Lloyd-Jones quotes George Frederick Handel (1685–1759) who wrote *The Messiah* in about three weeks and said, "I felt as if all heaven were open before me." "Our hymns are not Scripture," said Lloyd-Jones, "but that does not mean that they are not inspired."[2] Lloyd-Jones is right. He is not claiming that anyone could operate at the same level as the writers of the Bible. At most, they have God-given words as they write their poetry. The hymn writers are not explaining the progress of salvation-history and have no new doctrines to offer us. Nothing comes up to the prophetic heights of the Bible. In this connection we must emphasize that the whole Bible is prophetic.

Levels of prophecy: Prophetic preaching

We return to the theme of this book below. All I say here is this: preaching can be highly prophetic. Personally there are times when even as I am walking from a seat at the front of the church towards a pulpit or platform I have only the vaguest idea of what I am about to say. I often am still asking God to give me the right message. There have been times when even as I am looking at the Bible, seconds before I open its pages to expound it, I am not 100% sure what passage I shall be speaking from. I do not know what you want to call this, but personally, although in public I rarely call it anything other than preaching, I think of it as **prophetic** preaching. I do not say it happens all the time – it does not. But it happens a lot! My concern in this book is **not** to persuade anyone **not** to **study** God's Word. I personally read and study hundreds of Bible commentaries in English, French, Dutch and German – and work every day with piles of commentaries, and with Greek and Hebrew dictionaries all around me. My notes of my work run into millions of words in dozens of boxes. No one could possibly say I do not **prepare**! I am also often found pleading with preachers to learn Greek and Hebrew and have myself conducted classes in the biblical languages even for the "common people" in Chrisco Fellowship of Churches.[3] Yet it is still true that I believe that preaching has to be prophetic. The greatest blessings I have ever known in preaching have been "prepared" on a few scraps of paper, seconds before they were delivered. How do you think Peter "prepared" the preaching on the day of Pentecost? What kind of notes did he have, do you think? But we shall return to this theme shortly.

Levels of prophecy: Prophecy in times of trouble

There is one situation when we are all promised a gift of this kind. "When they deliver you over," said Jesus on one occasion, "do not be anxious how you are to speak or what you are to say, for what you are to say will be given to you in that hour." On another occasion He said something similar. "When they bring you to trial and deliver you over, do not be anxious beforehand what you are to say, but say whatever is given you in that hour, for it is not you who speak, but the Holy Spirit" (Matthew 10:19; Mark 13:11). The great Augustine made the point that if God can do this while we are in trouble He can also do it when we are preaching! God can "make us say what we ought, and in the way we ought". "Learn all that is to be taught ... But when the hour for speech arrives, let him reflect upon that saying of our Lord's . . ."[4] Luther also at times applied the same verse of Scripture to preaching.[5] But the major reference here is to times when God gives us what to say when we are in danger. "It is very remarkable," said Charles Spurgeon, "what wise answers many of the martyrs often gave. Illiterate men, when confronted by the learned ones of the earth, completely baffled them; and weak women nonplussed their assailants and judges."[6]

Low-level Prophecy

It is obvious that there is a kind of prophecy where God gives us what to say in a very remarkable manner. It is a mysterious thing and difficult to explain in words. It is not any kind of dictation. It is **not** a matter of God speaking to us and saying, "Say this" and we then repeat the words that He has dictated to us. There are times when we are using our own words – in our own style and with our own mannerisms! But somehow what we need to say comes out just right! It can happen in a committee meeting. It can happen in an important interview. It can happen at a time when we are witnessing to our friends or neighbours. And preachers should look to God for it to happen in their preaching!

What kind of trustworthiness or "infallibility" is found in prophecies of this nature? I would answer: it varies. At times God can surely give us inspirations and even tiny revelations of the future without making us infallibly correct either in content or in precise wording. In Caesarea, Agabus, a prophet who was visiting Caesarea from Jerusalem, dramatically and with prophetic symbolism warned Paul not to go to Jerusalem. This made the Christians plead with Paul to abandon his plans (21:12), but Paul would not be persuaded (21:13–14). Actually the prediction was not very precise and perhaps not quite correct. "The Jews at Jerusalem will bind the man who owns this belt and deliver him into the hands of the Gentiles," he said. In the event **Jewish** people tried to kill Paul; he was **rescued** by Roman soldiers as the mob cried, "Away with him!" – just as they had done to Jesus (Acts 21:30–36). Paul was carried, for safety, to the Roman barracks. So Agabus did not quite get it right! And Paul evidently did not feel he should take notice of him. It seems there is a kind of prophecy which might be roughly correct but is not 100% accurate.

Maybe there are yet further types of prophecy; I should think so. But my major concern is with preaching and I shall return to it soon.

Notes

1. J. Swanson, *Dictionary of Biblical Languages with Semantic Domains: Greek (New Testament)* (1997, electronic ed., Oak Harbor: Logos Research Systems, Inc.

2. D.M. Lloyd-Jones, *Westminster Record*, September 1968, p. 142. Charles Spurgeon spoke of "Handel with all the majesty of his half-inspired music . . ."! (Sermon 2204, in *Metropolitan Tabernacle Pulpit*, vol. 37).

3. See the details given in M.A. Eaton, *The Power of Prophetic Preaching* (ASL, 2005), pp. 42–47.

4. P. Schaff, *NPNF*, 1, vol. 2 [St. Augustin's City of God and Christian Doctrine], electronic edition (Oak Harbor: Logos Research Systems), p. 585. On the other hand Leo the Great warned against preachers misusing this text! See P. Schaff, *NPNF*, 2, vol. 12 [Leo the Great; Gregory the Great], electronic edition (Oak Harbor: Logos Research Systems), 118.

5. M. Luther, *LW*, 10 [First Lectures on the Psalms], (ed. J.J. Pelikan, H.C. Oswald & H.T. Lehmann), electronic edition, on Psalm 8:2.

6. C.H. Spurgeon, *MTP*, vol. 54, electronic edition (Logos Library System; Spurgeon's Sermons; Albany, OR; Ages Software). This comes in the exposition following sermon 3109.

Prophecy in Public Worship

Some good experiences

Perhaps this is the place where I might comment on prophecy as it is often found in charismatic churches in the public worship, especially on Sundays. Since the 1970s I have spent much of my life in charismatic churches (from a base in Chrisco Central Church, Nairobi, where I am one of its two pastors; and from Westminster Chapel, my home church when I am in London). I minister in such churches, preaching on average about seven times a week, and then getting involved in the follow-up and administration that comes as a result. Only infrequently have I preached in state-churches (Lutheran in Germany, Anglican in UK) and only occasionally in churches that are not specially "charismatic". In the charismatic churches I have now experienced hundreds of "personal prophecies" and hundreds of "prophetic words". But my impression is that the majority of these prophetic words do not turn out well. On the positive side there have been several occasions in my own life when I personally have been involved in or have received a "prophetic message" and it has turned out that it was obviously from God. There were two occasions when I left Zambia in 1977 when two different people gave me a kind of prediction of what would happen to me after I left the country. In the event I took ten months sabbatical leave in London to finish a commentary on *Ecclesiastes*, while at the same time looking for a new base in Africa from which to work. Both prophecies were precisely fulfilled and were exactly right. Both helped me considerably through a perplexing year in my life. Another "word from God" – a prophetic "picture" they called it – in Seaforth Evangelical Church (Surrey, UK), in 1981, gave me guidance and courage in building a multiracial fellowship in Johannesburg in the apartheid years in South Africa. A couple of decades later there was an occasion in a church in Bracknell (Surrey, UK) where I was given a "word from God" that I felt sure was right; I acted upon it, and it has given me clarity of thought to this day concerning one aspect of my work. There have been a few other – less important – occasions when I have felt that a message of this kind was truly from God, amounting to about ten in all. I have also known many occasions when such words have been given to other people and they have turned out well. I myself have occasionally given a word of advice (using language like "it seems to me", rather than "Thus says the Lord"!) which has turned out to be more God-given than I realized at the time.

But . . .

So I am not against "words from God" given in church meetings. But, on the other hand, most of them do not seem to turn out well! In my own life ten times in thirty years does not amount to much! On dozens of other occasions I have felt led by the Holy Spirit to take no notice of such messages whatsoever! I have heard hundreds of "prophecies" that have seemed to me to be disastrously in error. Even now as I write in Nairobi, Kenya, a presidential election is only a few weeks away, and the prophecies have been coming thick and fast about what is to happen in our land. True, they are getting less and less and the election-day gets nearer! When you are about to be proved right or wrong **tomorrow**, your boldness in giving prophecies subsides! But only a few weeks ago some "prophets" were telling us one presidential candidate would win the election. Another "prophet" was telling us that this man would succeed to the presidency. There are three main candidates so the prophets have a one in three chance of being right. I have some guesswork of my own (I do not call it anything else), but even as I write things are changing fast by the day and some unexpected events are taking place. There have been some surprising shifts and changes-of-party among some politicians. The swaps and changes get more surprising as the days go by, but none of them were mentioned in the "prophecies" of the various pastors in Nairobi! I have to say many of these prophecies seem to me to be guess-work or odd ideas floating through the mind which are thought to come from God! I cannot help but think of the terrifying things Jeremiah said about those who got their message only from their own imaginations. "They speak visions of their own minds," says Jeremiah. *"This is what Yahweh Almighty says, 'Do not listen to the words of the prophets who prophesy to you, filling you with vain hopes. They speak visions of their own minds, not from the mouth of Yahweh'"* (Jeremiah 23:16). Their messages were simply a matter of what people liked to hear. But they had not had the prophetic experience of knowing they are in the presence of God and that God is giving them revelations from Himself. *"For who among them has stood in the council of Yahweh and has seen and heard his word? Who has paid attention to his word and listened?"* (23:18).

God gets angry about public figures pretending to have a word from Him but whose words comes from their own imaginations. *"Behold, the storm of Yahweh!"* (23:19). True prophecy has its source in a call from God. *"I did not send these prophets, yet they ran; I did not speak to them, yet they prophesied. If they had stood my council, they would have announced my words to my people, and then they would have turned them from their evil way, and from the evil of their deeds"* (23:21–22).

The false prophets were not sent by God; the true prophet is. The false prophets were claiming to have instructions from God but it was simply a lie. True ministry begins with the sure knowledge that we are being compelled with a holy compulsion. Unless you are sent by God you cannot be a spiritual leader of this kind. All the more reason why we should hear God's voice and know our calling.

The prophetic in our churches

We are often asked to "make room for the prophetic" in churches today. To what extent, we might ask, is this a good and valid appeal? I answer as follows. When the "Charismatic Movement" began in the 1960s, many of us listened to arguments asking us to go back to the New Testament and include prophecy in the Church. It was said, "the gift of prophecy can still continue in the Church." I was convinced this was right and so were many others. The little booklet, *Prophecy: A Gift for the Body of Christ* (1964) by Michael Harper of Fountain Trust (who subsequently joined the Greek Orthodox Church!) was pondered by many of us line by line. The Bible clearly allows that prophecy can continue to the end of the gospel age. At first some were wanting to say, "But the **office** of a prophet does not continue." Lloyd-Jones said something like this. The **office** (that is, the recognised position with its accompanying status) of a prophet has ceased but the **gift** continues, we were told. Then a little later this was thought to be inconsistent. If the gift continues then there is no reason to think that we might not have "prophets" in the Church. Later still people began to wonder if the apostolic gift might also still exist. There were people who were willing to use the word **apostolic** of current-day ministry but not the word **apostle**. Even John Stott of All Souls, Langham Place, London (well known for his dislike of the Charismatic Movement) spoke of "the adjective but not the noun"! But by "apostolic" he only meant "based on the New Testament". By some people the adjective was allowed but the noun was forbidden!

However, what happened in many circles was that both apostles and prophets were still thought possible in the life of the Church. I personally went along with all of this, and myself joined a "five-fold ministry" – Christ's Co-Workers Fellowship in Nairobi.

However, now that several decades have gone by we are in a position where we might ask, "How does the prophetic look to us after forty years or more of trying to encourage it?" Personally, I have three convictions about the matter at the present stage of my life.

We have not entirely succeeded in keeping balance and wisdom in our churches. Of course "keeping balance and wisdom" is never easy in a movement of the Holy Spirit. It did not happen in Corinth and it will not happen with us if God the Holy Spirit really moves in power. We shall make mistakes, but better to make mistakes than to remain in the neat, tidy orderliness of a graveyard or cemetery. He who makes no mistakes never makes anything!

Seeing miraculous gifts in the Bible is one thing. Keeping balance and wisdom in our churches is something else. We have taken a lot of risks and churches open to the Holy Spirit have experienced "a little reviving" over recent decades and sometimes more than a little! True, we have not turned western nations back to Christian faith as happened in the eighteenth century and in nineteenth-century America. But some good things have happened. Where would the world be if there had been no Charismatic Movement? And we can be sure that greater things are yet to happen in the kingdom of God.

However, we all make mistakes and it is clear, in my judgement, that we have allowed under the heading of "prophecy" a lot that should not have been allowed.

We need meetings in our churches where all Christians may contribute. Although I believe preaching at its best is prophetic, I do not suggest that prophetic preaching is the **total** range of the gift of prophecy, and somewhere in the life of our churches we need fellowship meetings where everyone can contribute. It is sometimes said, "There must be room for the prophetic in our church meetings." This is true, but I do not think we should put it quite like that! Why do we have to **announce in advance** what God is going to do? Are we in control of God? Can we switch on prophecy? If a meeting is open to all sorts of gifting something might happen which we recognize as being "inspired" in some way, but we would be wise not to announce in advance that prophecies are about to come! It will lead to people who like to think their talk is supernatural becoming too eager to speak. Open your meetings to "the prophetic" and you will soon see what I mean. There should surely be times in our churches when people can contribute all sorts of items: a piece of teaching that means much to someone, a five-minute comment upon a Scripture that has helped us, a testimony of a recent experience, the story of someone who has just come to salvation. There are dangers in this kind of thing and the churches must make it clear that they are not wanting nothing but endless healing-stories with the end of every bit of sickness treated as a miracle! Nor do we want endless stories of promotion and how God helped someone get rich! Money stories should not be the endless theme of "testimony time". Prophecy is a very wide gift. It will perhaps show itself when we give room for it, but we have to guard against that which does not build up the Church. That might take time. The Church might have to be taught what is and is not edifying. Non-preaching prophecy will be part of such meetings. Prophecy is obviously a very wide gift. There can even be prophetic chit-chat! There can be prophecies where in a single sentence some-one says something that changes the entire life of a congregation.

But still our great need is prophetic biblical expository preaching. This is the theme of my book! However, I hasten to add even this must not become an extremism. We must not worship preaching. We must not so elevate preaching that our churches do nothing else. Certainly the kind of church that becomes more like a university with its preachers becoming expository **lecturers** with everyone scribbling notes – has something missing! The preaching is high on our agenda, but it is only a means to an end; it is not an end in itself. Its aim is to move God's people into assurance of salvation, into lives of spirituality and godliness, into every-member ministry, into living for the glory of God. The test of our preaching is whether it is actually happening and whether churches are moving into living for the glory of God!

It is this kind of prophetic preaching that brings revival and renewed liveliness to the churches. It is not preaching in the ordinary sense (what goes on in pulpits, religious discourse to a closed group of initiates, loose chit-chat that quotes the Bible and gives moral exhortation) but something altogether more powerful, convicting and life-changing. The New Testament calls it "prophecy". The Lord Jesus Christ promised His disciples that He would send them His Holy Spirit who would empower them to bear witness to Him in the world, and would bear witness with them. Those who preached the gospel at the first did so in the power of the "Holy Spirit sent from heaven". Often there were amazing side-effects and manifestations of power. Every Christian is **potentially** a prophet (as Moses wanted, according to Numbers 11:29). Paul tells us to "earnestly desire the spiritual gifts, especially that you may prophesy." When this is combined with what the New Testament calls "heralding" or "preaching", the ministry of the churches to the world goes forward.

Protecting the Flock

I am a believer then in the continuing gift of prophecy, but in recent years we have tended to make the mistakes that re-discoverers of prophecy nearly always make!

Extremism

Whenever there is a renewed interest in prophetic gifts there are always weird extremists who bring discredit to the whole idea of the living voice of God. We think of Montanism which arose as a kind of "Pentecostal" movement toward the close of the second century. Tertullian, its greatest supporter, was firmly of the opinion that the gospel was fixed and needed no additions. He believed that the need of continued supernatural revelations had to do with matters of duty and discipline. But it was not long before Montanism went astray and started adding new doctrines concerning the Second Coming of Christ. It developed a denunciatory and exclusive spirit and was soon condemned by the other churches.

We think too of George Fox and the early Quakers of the seventeenth century. George Fox himself, despite all his eccentricities, was undoubtedly a man full of the Holy Spirit. But it was not long before one of the early Quakers – James Naylor, a sincere man – was so deluded by what he thought was a revelation from God, he rode a horse into the City of Bristol claiming that he was the Messiah! Some weird things happen as the result of men and women thinking the Spirit of God is speaking to them! Lloyd-Jones mentions the case of the barrister Robert Baxter who was ready to leave his wife, children and his career because of a supposed "revelation" he had received – until he realised his revelation was not from the Holy Spirit at all![1] As people who like to see the prophetic restored we would do well to have in our minds a list of what will definitely not help the congregation and make sure that the congregation knows that certain eccentric styles of so-called prophecy will not be encouraged. I mention a few of them.

Introspection?

Prophecy is not weepy, tearful, introspection! There is a certain kind of person who loves talk about prophecy because it seems to give a chance to a certain kind of introspective emotionalism that they love. They like talk about inner healing and want emphasis on finding peace and having God soothe our souls. I well remember a man who, when I was once attending a meeting where I was not well-known, came to me with a "word from the Lord". As far as I remember it was something like this: "God has told me," he said to me, "that if you were to lie prostrate on this cold stone floor [it was in a searingly hot time in India!] God will answer your prayers and you will enter into rich blessing." He had a lot of people lying on the floor and wanted me to join them! He did not know I was a preacher (people of this kind do not do this to preachers, so much! They like quiet, shy people, like me when I'm not preaching! Later on after he had heard me preach he left me alone!)

There are many objections to this kind of allegedly prophetic ministry. It tends to be highly subjective, whereas the Bible begins with the objective. It keeps us looking at ourselves so much and when it talks about God it makes God so nice and friendly as to be unlike the God of the Bible – who is not maudlin or syrupy or "comforting" in an overindulgent manner. The God of the Bible talks more about what He is doing in history than what He is doing in our psyche! When we have our little aches and pains He is likely to say to us, *"If you have raced with men on foot, and they have wearied you, how will you compete with horses? And if in a safe land you fall down, what will you do in the hilly terrain near the Jordan?"* God's answer to us is likely to be to tell us to be tough. Things might get even worse! The encouragement of the Bible is virile and strong. We lift up our eyes to a mighty God. We look away from ourselves and are not very bothered about our emotional state. Our light, momentary afflictions cease to bother us in the light of God's exceeding weight of glory! The word of God brings us rich spiritual experience, but it is not of the maudlin, syrupy type. The type of so-called prophetic word I have in mind wants us to look at ourselves in a wrong way. It wants us to be supremely concerned about ourselves. When the Spirit comes upon us in fullness all our little aches and pains of the soul seem to disappear. When God speaks in power to us it **rescues** us from introspection.

There is a certain kind of counselling style in the Church which likes to call itself "prophetic" but personally I call weepy, tearful, introspection! It likes to gives personal prophecies. Its idea of a successful meeting is that everyone is lying on the floor weeping. I personally do not think we should go down this route. I admit that sometimes God moves in such power that everyone collapses in tears, but if this is really from God it is not organised or manipulated. It comes as a surprise! Organising prophetic meetings of the weepy, tearful, introspective kind is something different. Of course, some people love it. Their idea of being touched by God is to have a good cry. But this is operating at the level of the psychological, not at the level of the Holy Spirit. There is a difference between having a good weep and being touched by the Spirit.

Israel?

Prophecy is not guess-work about the nation of Israel. This kind of prophecy does not come so much in our meetings for prayer, but I mention it under this heading. What a lot of nonsense is spilled out in predictions about what is going to happen in Israel. How often the second edition of a "prophetic" book has to quietly drop what was said in the first edition. How easy it is for pagan people to ridicule the churches, if they know anything of these extremists. People like Nicholas Guyatt (I refer to his *Have a Nice Doomsday*) ridicule the Christians for their disastrous false predictions about Israel, and some of us feel like agreeing with him! Some "prophecies" are positively dangerous; dogmatically insisting Iran will use nuclear weapons against the USA leads easily into encouraging a pre-emptive nuclear strike. Do we really want such prophecies in our churches?

Prediction?

Prophecy is not generally telling people details about their future. Actually there is often a basic misunderstanding of the verb "prophesy" at this point. There are people who think the word "prophesy" means "predict". We do sometimes use the word in this way. The average English dictionary will give "predict" as one of the meanings of "prophesy". But remember that the Bible is a translation of documents in Hebrew, in Aramaic (in 268 verses) and in Greek. The question is not what the English word means but what do the underlying biblical words mean? It has to be said that prediction is not an essential part of prophesying. You can be prophesying even when what you are not saying does not include anything predictive at all. Prophecy **may** be predictive. We think of how Isaiah foretold that the conqueror of Babylon would be someone named "Cyrus" hundreds of years before Cyrus appeared. So dramatic is the prediction that some have to say that maybe this bit of Isaiah was written a few hundred years later than Isaiah son of Amoz who lived in eighth-century BC Jerusalem. They find it difficult to cope with the idea that there could be such a dramatic prediction. Personally I do not have these problems and have no doubts that Isaiah son of Amoz predicted Cyrus by name! But still it remains true that not all prophesying is predictive and that the word "prophesy", in biblical language, does not mean "predict".

The need of the hour

My assessment of the need of the hour is this. **Prophetic expository preaching** is our great need. Other forms of "prophesying" need to be subordinate to the prophetic exposition of the Word of God more than ever. Am I saying that prophecy is simply what is today called "preaching"? No, I am not. The sixteenth-century Reformers of the Church (Luther, Zwingli, Calvin and others) tended to say that, but I am not agreeing with them. Nor am I saying that prophetic preaching is the **totality** of what is meant by the word "prophecy". Not at all! Prophecy is surely a wide and broad gift. No, what is needed is the particular mixture of gifts that I call prophetic expository preaching. It must have God-given power. It must be expository – at least in the loose sense that it arises out of the total gospel message found in Scripture. It must be "preaching" – *kērussōn* – a public proclamation of the gospel. This is the greatest gift (prophecy) plus the greatest message (the gospel) plus the greatest activity (proclamation from God). We need it, and so does the world.

So my recommendation for "worship leaders" or those with church meetings in their care is this: (i) In the main, public services put prophetic preaching high on the agenda and give plenty of time for it. I usually ask for at least 45 minutes and prefer about 55 – and more when God is obviously present in power. (ii) Have times within church life when all can participate, but such meetings may have to be gently steered. Things have to be done decently and in order. Charismatic chaos must not be allowed to run into wildness or extremism or false teaching. (iii) There is perhaps no way of controlling the "prophetic nuisance" – the man or woman who likes hearing his own voice and loves morbid, introspective, demonic or over-exciting themes. They have to be dealt with **at the time** in a loving manner, and maybe again **after the event**. (iv) Worship-leaders (or whoever) do well just to **chat casually** about what is and is to be allowed in such meetings. Gentle hints will normally be enough. If the prophetic nuisance continues something more drastic may have to be done. If such meetings have to be curtailed for a few weeks and **then** brought back, some words of explanation need to be given.

The important thing is to keep a balance. There must be every-member participation in the life of the church. Yet at the same time there must be the "systematic-yet-inspired" exposition of the Word of God, and church life must arise out of what we learn from God's Word, neither more nor less.

Notes

1. D.M. Lloyd-Jones, *Romans: Christian Conduct* – Romans 12 (Banner of Truth, 2000), p. 249.

CHAPTER 5

Howell Harris,
Edwin Hatch,
Martyn Lloyd-Jones

Howell Harris of Trevecca

Take the case of Howell Harris, the eighteenth-century preacher. He was nervous about claiming to be any kind of preacher and would only call himself an "exhorter". He would try to help people in eighteenth-century Wales at first by reading to them from books. But then as he was reading he would add words of his own. People would come to hear him and the crowds got larger. His reading gradually turned into prophetic preaching! Eventually he had to preach in the open air to the crowds that wanted to hear him. He would speak almost entirely in a spontaneous manner. "I took no particular text but discoursed freely as the Lord gave me utterance," he said. "[I]t was all given to me in an extraordinary manner without the least premeditation." This preaching of Howell Harris had extraordinary power. "The Word was attended with much power that many on the spot cried out to God for pardon of their sins." Harris also said, "In all my discourses, before the power comes I open the contexts." What this means is that he began simply by coolly and calmly expounding the total passage he was considering (if he did indeed have a text), but then there would come a point where he would feel led to press a particular point upon the people. At that point he would be very conscious of the presence of the Holy Spirit. He would trust entirely in God's power on such occasions. "I wondered where the words come from, so clear, so prolific, so appropriate," he said. He could preach all day doing this – sometimes for as much as nine hours without weariness! "I feared that pride might rise in my heart, so extraordinary was the gift." Gradually Howell Harris matured in his gift and would use more of the exposition of Scripture and put his material under headings. But still he exercised this gift; I would call it prophetic preaching.[1]

The argument of Edwin Hatch

Consider the argument of Edwin Hatch. I do not mention him as any kind of prophet, but as a biblical scholar. Hatch, who lived and worked in the early twentieth century maintained that in the early Christian churches public ministry was a matter of "prophesying". "[The] prophet" he said, "was not merely a preacher but a spontaneous preacher...[2] They did not practise beforehand how or what they should say ... The greatest preacher of all [Paul] claimed to have come among his converts, in a city in which rhetoric flourished, not with the persuasiveness of human logic, but with the demonstration which was afforded by spiritual power...[3] In the course of the second century, this original spontaneity of utterance died almost entirely away. It may almost be said to have died a violent death...[4] In place of prophesying came preaching...".[5] In other words, teaching and exposition of the received doctrine plus ethical exhortation came in instead of the original more prophetic speaking. Hatch continues, "It is this [later] form of teaching and exhortation that constituted the essence of the homily."[6] Eventually, he says, "The voice of the prophet had ceased, and the voice of the preacher had begun."[7] Hatch pointed out that, "The greatest Christian preachers of the fourth century had been trained to rhetorical methods, and had themselves taught rhetoric." They all tended to have the **same** artificiality of structure in their sermons and a similarity of phraseology.[8] Eventually, the "preachers preached, not because they were bursting with truths which could not help finding expression, but because they were masters of fine phrases and lived in an age in which fine phrases had a value."[9]

What do we have to say to all of this? **I would say that it is correct in which it affirms but wrong in what it denies.** The basic point that Hatch asserts – that early Christian public preaching was largely spontaneous – seems indisputable. Peter obviously did not have time to prepare for the sermon of Acts 2 in the sense of writing out a sermon! The exhortation of Jesus, *"Take heed of covetousness . . . "* (Luke 12:15) and the "parable of the rich fool" was (as Luke presents it) entirely spontaneous. Jesus was preaching mainly about the Pharisees (see Luke 11:37, 45; 12:1). Suddenly a man shouts out from the crowd, *"Tell my brother to divide the inheritance with me"* he calls out. While Jesus is preaching, the man is thinking about a family quarrel in which his brother will not release a share of the family wealth. Jesus is speaking about judgement day and the danger of a sin that is eternally unforgiven, but the man in the crowd is thinking about money! He is one of many who have the idea that the Christian faith is all about making our earthly life easier.

But Jesus answers bluntly. *"Who appointed me a judge or divider over you?"* (12:14). He is spontaneously responding to what has just happened. None of it was in his "sermon notes". It leads Jesus on to talk further about money. Anxiety is needless. Life is bigger than possessions (12:22–23). God will give what is needed without our striving. The ravens are fed without anxiety; the same care of God that feeds them will feed God's people (12:24). Worry cannot achieve anything (12:25) – and so on. It all arose out of one's man's remark shouted out amidst the crowd. Is not this prophetic preaching? Verse 26 (which has no parallel in Matthew) makes the point that since they cannot add the tiniest unit to one's length of life why not simply do what has to be done but leave all the strain to God. God adequately clothes flowers; He will even more clothe His people (12:27–28). The disciples must be a contrast to godless people (12:29–30a). They must trust in God's knowledge (12:30b) and must have their attention elsewhere in seeking the kingdom which God is eager to give them (12:31–32). They must be generous to others (12:33a) and lay up rewards in heaven (12:33b). The supreme delight of their life – whether it is money or God's kingdom – will captivate their "heart". If money is the delight of their life, their hearts will be earthbound. Let them make God and His kingdom to be their precious treasure (12:34).[10] After the "parable of the rich fool" Jesus follows up His story with direct teaching in which He urges His disciples to freedom from anxiety (12:22–34), readiness in His service (12:35–40), and to faithfulness (12:41–48).

I call this prophetic preaching – spontaneous God-given speaking that is directly relevant to what is happening at the very moment when the message is being given. It is of course quite likely that Jesus had said these things many times before. It is not necessary to think that every thought is coming to Him for the first time ever in His life! In this sense His message may well have been "prepared" – but still it was coming to the crowds with God-given immediacy, God-given inspiration, and God-given authority.

But I believe that Edwin Hatch is mistaken in what he seems to deny (that the sermons of the early preachers had no structure). There is obvious a closely argued logic in the sermon on the Day of Pentecost. Prophetic power does not destroy logical ability, it enhances it!

The case of Dr Lloyd-Jones

The preaching of Dr Lloyd-Jones often also had this "prophetic" touch too. He also could respond to what was happening as it was happening. When a man shouted out "Amen" in the middle of one of his sermons on the new birth, "the doctor" did not ignore it. Instead he made use of it. He was very conscious that the Spirit of God is often at work in the material that the preacher has **not** been prepared. He said on that occasion: "Constantly one is being told that some side glancing remark has been the very thing that the Spirit has used to bring such-and-such a person to a knowledge of the truth. The minister rightly prepares his sermon; he has order; he has logic; he has development; and his danger of course is to think that it is that that is going to do the work. No it isn't! That's merely the scaffolding; the Spirit does the work. And one is therefore often humbled and corrected by finding that something that one merely said as an aside is the very thing that is used of God . . . It is this other element – this other spiritual element that really matters above everything else." He went on to warn even against the taking notes of sermons lest the power should be missed in the eagerness to gain knowledge! "Be careful," he said, "lest while you are taking notes you are missing something of the Spirit himself." He hated the thought of making preaching something merely academic.

On the occasion I refer to, suddenly, in the midst of the sermon someone called out "Amen". Lloyd-Jones instantly commented on it: "Well, I don't know that you should say 'Amen' to that! That was a bit of self-righteousness, I think, whoever said it! It was a self-righteous remark! But I am just emphasizing that the Spirit is more important than the knowledge here, and that is where this realm is altogether different from every other realm . . . "[11] It was this kind of immediate response to the moment that brought such a sense of power in Lloyd-Jones' ministry.

He could respond to dull singing and, on the spur of the moment, incorporate a comment on it into his preaching when a hymn was badly sung by the congregation. At Westminster Chapel in 1959 he began a message concerning revival by commenting on the song that had just been sung.

> "If I'd had any doubts before as to whether this particular message was really needed they would certainly all have gone after listening to the way in which you've just been singing that hymn . . . ! Did you notice how we sang it? We dragged it mournfully."

And then he began to mimic the slow depressed way in which the song had been sung!

" 'Cast . . . thy . . . dreams . . . of . . . ease . . . away . . . thou . . . are . . . in . . . the . . . midst . . . of . . . foes . . . Watch . . .and . . .pray . . . ' Exactly! And that is why the church is as she is. That was a call to arms, to watchfulness to vigilance, to gird ourselves with armour! It wasn't a lament! But thus I say the church seems to have been overcome by such a spirit of lethargy and of defeatism, and thereby she gives the impression to those who are outside that she is filled with a sense of despair. We even drag a call to arms, and are mournful as we remind ourselves of the armour in which we can place a final confidence and trust . . . We need very badly what Isaiah has to tell us . . . "

Such remarks were never in Lloyd-Jones' notes, never part of what he had planned to say. He would say such things spontaneously, following the leading of the Spirit in the very moment when something happened that would call them forth.[12]

The best way to define prophecy – thought Dr Lloyd-Jones – is to compare and contrast it with teaching and preaching. There is a difference "and the difference can be put in one word – immediacy . . . Prophecy is something that is given to someone immediately and directly." It is "a direct revelation". Dr Lloyd-Jones was a very self-effacing man in many ways but a close look at his words shows that he quite distinctly claims to have this gift himself (as he undoubtedly did). "I think I know just a little about this," he said. "I think I know something of what it is to be preaching or teaching, and suddenly to find myself prophesying. I am aware that my words are not what I prepared, but have been given at that moment, and with clarity and force and directness. I am speaking, and am listening to myself, as it were, because it is not me." Such impulses and giftings have to be safeguarded – said Lloyd-Jones. They are not "revelation" in the sense that the Scripture writers were given revelation, but still there is such a thing as a revelation of the Word of God coming with unusual immediacy and directness.

Expository preaching! I am a great believer in it, but the emphasis must be on the second word not the first! There is a lot that goes under the name of expository preaching that I believe should be called popular expository lecturing. I do not doubt that it is useful but one can scarcely call it prophetic. I can forgive a man whose preaching is not accurate, balanced and with a steady exposition. I can forgive a man whose exegesis is not 100% accurate. But I can hardly forgive a man for speaking the Word of God without prophetic fire, without any immediacy, without any feeling that what he is saying, God is saying. "We have tended," said Dr Lloyd-Jones on another occasion, "to become so tied to exegesis and exposition, pure and simple, that we think that when we have expounded a verse or a passage then we have truly preached."[13] But it is not so. It is a common downgrading of the word "preach". When Alan Richardson give his eight Bampton Lectures in 1962 on *History Sacred and Profane*, he called what he did "preaching"[14] but one can scarcely imagine anything less like New Testament preaching – "not only in word, but also in power and in the Holy Spirit and with full conviction" – than Alan Richardson's Bampton Lectures – magnificent though they are as academic addresses.

Notes

1. See D.M. Lloyd-Jones, Howell Harris and Revival, *The Puritans* (Banner of Truth, 1987), pp. 282–302.
2. E. Hatch, *The Influence of Greek Ideas and Usages Upon the Christian Church* (London & Edinburgh, 1901), pp. 105–106.
3. Hatch, *Influence*, p. 106.
4. Hatch, *Influence*, pp. 106–107.
5. Hatch, *Influence*, p. 107.
6. Hatch, *Influence*, p. 108.
7. Hatch, *Influence*, p. 109.
8. See Hatch, *Influence*, p. 112.
9. Hatch, *Influence*, p. 113.
10. I am aware of the scholars who will say this is Luke's grouping of material together which originally came from different settings. There **might occasionally** be editing of the material in this manner; it is obviously so in Luke 4:16–30. But I have argued elsewhere that the chronological sequence of Mark, Luke and John is generally to be taken seriously and only in Matthew is there **demonstrably** much of this kind of editing. Luke 12 is itself evidence in the opposite direction; obviously there is a connection between Luke 12:14 and what follows, and the connection is historical not merely literary. See further, M.A. Eaton, *The Jesus of the Gospels* (New Wine, 2007).

11. Lloyd-Jones Recording Trust, sermon 1123, on John 3:1–8.

12. The printed version of the sermon smooths out this rebuke to the congregation and makes it a more general comment. See D.M. Lloyd-Jones; *Revival* (Marshall Pickering, 1986), p. 250.

13. D.M. Lloyd-Jones, *The Puritans* (Banner of Truth, 1987), p. 387.

14. A. Richardson, *History Sacred and Profane*, Bampton Lectures, 1962, (SCM, 1964), p. 13.

II. Preparing for the Prophetic?

CHAPTER 6

Some Technicalities First

The question we shall want to ask, then, is: can we prepare for the prophetic? In one respect the answer is no! The directness and immediacy of prophetic words are such that there is no preparation for the exercise of such a gift. But on the other hand what I am calling prophetic preaching functions at its best when it draws upon a background of knowledge and spiritual understanding.

Charles Spurgeon (1834–1892) – the most effective prophetic preacher of nineteenth century Britain – is a good example of this very point. He could speak very spontaneously and without preparation. He could suddenly be given something to say from God seconds before he started speaking. But it would be a great mistake to think that he did not prepare himself for a ministry of preaching. He kept a library of 12,000 books. He studied day and night. "Bees are making honey from morning till night, and we should be always gathering stores for our people," he said. "I have no belief in that ministry which ignores laborious preparation."[1]

Different people have different ministries and it would be a mistake for me to make rules about how prophetic preachers should prepare for their work. There will be different interests, different aptitudes, different callings for each preacher. All I can do at the moment is make a list of the kind of work that has to be done somewhere and somehow for the use of the prophetic preacher. He may not do that precise work himself. The work of proclaiming Scripture is a **collective** task. Even when we read a Bible in the

English language we are making use of work that someone else has done. A lot of the preparation for the work of preaching is done by other people. But there is much to be said for having it clear in our minds what work has to be done for the Word of God to be prophetically preached in power.

The Old Testament text

Before we can preach from the Scriptures we must have a grasp of them; we must have expositions of them in our own minds. But even that is not the beginning. Before we can get at the **message** of the Bible we must have a basic understanding of what I must call "the technicalities" of Bible-reading. Three of them confront us the very moment we open our Bibles. They are matters of text, of basic interpretation and of translation.

I begin with the "textual criticism" of the Old Testament. The Old Testament was written mainly in Hebrew; between two and three hundred verses were written in Aramaic. The original documents were no doubt written on leather parchments made from animal skins. Only the consonants were written. An ancient scribe could see a word written *dbr* and know at a glance that it was the word *dabar* ("word"). Further copies of the books would be produced by their being copied by scribes. The original documents have not survived. Before 1947 manuscripts of the Old Testament books were never to be dated earlier than the ninth century AD. Then the discovery in 1947 of the Dead Sea Scrolls in a place called Qumran involved the finding of manuscripts a thousand years older than any that had been known before that time.

The copying of the manuscripts again and again led to small errors of copying being made, and so Old Testament scholars have to study the various manuscripts so as to find out what mistakes have been made and as much as possible reconstruct the original text. That is to say, our manuscripts have "variant readings" and scholars have to work out in any particular case what is the correct reading. Ancient scholars did this work very thoroughly and by the end of the fifth century there was already a standard text which was incredibly accurate and well preserved. The scholars who did this work are called Masoretes (a Hebrew word meaning "transmitters") and the Hebrew text of the Old Testament used by scholars today is called the Masoretic Text (often abbreviated as MT). It is a marvellous text. The Jewish scribes exercised great care in copying their sacred books. Among other things the Masoretes introduced vowel signs into the Hebrew Bible and so made clear and visible what should be the pronunciation of words. They left the original consonantal text unchanged and mentioned any queries they had in textual notes, placed in the margin. When printing was invented in the fifteenth century, Jewish printers began putting into print portions of the Hebrew Old Testament. The entire Hebrew and Aramaic text was first published in 1488.

What does all this have to do with the prophetic preacher? The answer is that every Christian needs to know about textual variants. The Hebrew text which modern translations use is the Masoretic text of the Hebrew Bible as found in various modern publications. There is good reason to believe that it is incredibly reliable. But inevitably there is the possibility that in tiny matters it might be possible to improve the text. As copies of the original were made it could happen that tiny textual variations would arise in the Hebrew manuscripts. As the manuscripts were recopied variations among the manuscripts crept in. An "R" could look like a "D". The Hebrew for "witnesses" (with a Hebrew D) looked like the Hebrew for "cities" (with a Hebrew R). "Covenants are broken; **cities** are despised" – says the ESV of Isaiah 33:8. But the NIV says, "The treaty is broken, its **witnesses** are despised". Why does one have "cities" but the other has "witnesses"? The answer is: in Hebrew "cities" is *'ry* (omitting the vowels); "witnesses" is *'dy*. The R and the D looked almost the same. There is evidence that some manuscripts read *'dy*; the Masoretic text has *'ry*. So there is a variant reading.

The Hebrew Old Testament was translated in early times into some of the ancient languages. A Greek translation was made in the third century BC. In Israel people began to speak Aramaic and needed an Aramaic paraphrase of the Hebrew text. These "targums" (paraphrases) were initially only oral, but later they were written down. These translations and some later ones, including those in Latin and in Syriac are important in establishing the correct text of the Old Testament. Scholars use them to find evidence as to what was the Hebrew text at the time these translations were being made.

For much of the time, and for all practical purposes, the ordinary Christian need not bother about textual variants so long as a reliable translation is being used. But Old Testament scholars have tended in the past to "emend" the Hebrew text excessively. When the text is difficult they have often held the view that the Hebrew text needs improving. They often consult ancient translations and translate them back into Hebrew to see what Hebrew the translators had before them. The MT and the translations are used to get back to the original.

Now what is the importance of all this for the ordinary Christian who knows little about ancient languages? And of what importance is it for the prophetic preacher? Well, I say only one thing. The preacher has to know enough about this subject to know whether what he is reading really is the Word of God. In practise it means that we must use translations which do not "emend the text" too much. Some versions of the Bible are only too willing to see copying errors in our Old Testament. In point of fact our MT is incredibly reliable (and scholars have come to appreciate it more than they did a century ago). We need to use translations which handle the Hebrew text with care and emend the text only when there is clear evidence that it is possible to improve on the MT. Some of the scholars' work was done in an unsatisfactory manner in the nineteenth century, and even today we need to be aware of which scholars and translations handle the text in a sceptical manner. In the New English Bible (NEB), for example, there are about 90 emendations in the book of Hosea, just under half of them based on ancient translations and just over half of them based on intelligent guesswork. But this is quite unsatisfactory. What Christian wants to be treating as the Word of God a translation from Hebrew of something that does not exist in any manuscript in the world, but was invented by some scholar a few years ago? Textual criticism is a necessary task – there is no doubt about that – but it has to be done with better principles than have been followed in the last century or so. For this reason it is important to use Old Testament translations that do not follow speculations in their translation work. One test of a good translation for a Christian who is looking at Scripture as God's Word is how it handles the Old Testament textual difficulties. Translations like the NEB, the Revised English Bible (REB), the New American Bible (NAB, a catholic work not to be confused with the New American Standard Bible), the Jerusalem Bible (JB), the Good News Bible (GNB), and others have a high quantity of emendations. Often the scholar writes his own Hebrew text before he translates it! One needs to be on surer ground than this. The consonantal Hebrew text passed down by the Masoretes has signs of great accuracy. It should only be emended in its consonantal readings where there are very substantial reasons for doing so. Even the vowel-pointing of the MT is surprisingly reliable and should not be lightly emended.

The most reliable handy translations for detailed study of the Bible are the New International Version (NIV), the New American Standard Bible (NASB) and the English Standard Version (ESV). Also the English Revised Version (RV) of 1881 and 1885 was a very accurate translation, especially in its American version known as the American Standard Version (1901). Since the 1960s about a dozen translations have been competing for popularity. The NASB is very accurate but does not read well in public. The ESV does better in this respect. The NIV reads well, but it breaks away from the tradition of the old King James or Authorised Version (KJV/AV) in a way that gives it a slightly foreign atmosphere in Christian circles dominated by the AV tradition. If the accuracy of the NASB could be combined with greater literary sensitivity we would have a near-perfect English Bible. At the moment, English speaking Christians have the NIV, the ESV and the NASB as the best modern translations for detailed study.

Certainly a preacher of the Bible needs to know that what he is preaching on really is in the biblical text! Nowadays more is known of Semitic languages and some difficulties in the Hebrew text have received explanation that was not available at the time of pre-twentieth-century translations. Scholars are nowadays less happy with slapdash and indiscriminate emendations. This is a much more satisfactory procedure than excessive and unrestrained emendations. The Masoretic text (MT) of the Old Testament is the superior text. Only rarely can it be improved and the suggested changes need to be evaluated carefully. The MT was copied with extraordinary care. The Masoretes kept detailed statistics of each book of the Old Testament. For example, they noted that Deuteronomy has 955 verses, that its middle point occurs in 17:10 and the Hebrew text consists of 5,845 verses, 79,856 words and 400,945 letters. These Masoretic comments were a way of checking manuscripts. Any manuscript of Deuteronomy which did **not** have 400,945 letters contained a copying error! I cannot imagine how they did the work that went into maintaining these statistics in each manuscript. But it seems they did! The textual skills of the ancient Hebrew scribes are certainly the most efficient ever to be known.

Maybe the preacher does not have to do all this work, but someone somewhere must do it and the preacher must know about it!

The New Testament text

We must also be aware of the "textual criticism" of the New Testament. This is a simpler matter for the preacher than the case of the Old Testament. The New Testament was originally written by about nine people perhaps with assistants and editors: Matthew, Mark, Luke, John, Paul, James, Peter, Jude and the author of Hebrews. They would have written the originals on papyrus, a tall reed-plant, cut into strips and glued together in such a way that it can be used as a page for writing. Copies of the original manuscripts of the New Testament were made by scribes and eventually the number of hand-made copies amounted to thousands. There are still in existence over 5,300 manuscripts of the Greek New Testament or part of it, in the world's various museums and archives. Also there more than 8,000 manuscript copies of the ancient Latin New Testament, and hundreds of manuscript copies of other ancient translations. No other piece of ancient literature has such an abundance of manuscript witnesses as does the New Testament. The oldest known manuscript contains only John 18:31–33, 37–38, dating from the beginning of the second century. Modern printed editions of the Greek New Testament are not based on any one New Testament manuscript, but rather are the work of scholars seeking to reconstruct the original on the basis of the evidence of all known manuscripts. Translations of the sixteenth century were generally based on only a small number of manuscripts, but modern printed editions of the Greek New Testament seek to take them all into account as much as is possible. There is no identity between any commonly used Greek New Testament and any specific manuscript. Because of tiny copying errors and changes, no two Greek New Testament manuscripts are 100% identical. However, the task of textual criticism – establishing the right readings – is well advanced and over 90% of the variations have been clarified and we can generally be sure we have the exact words the original authors wrote. The errors of scribes can be studied and different types of mistakes corrected. Apart from deliberate changes, several types of error are well-known: **haplography** – writing once something that is actually repeated in the text; **dittography** – accidentally repeating what should only be found once; **false recollection or harmonisation** – inserting something from a passage elsewhere; **homoeoteleuton** – missing out a portion between two similar bits of script; **line omission** – skipping a line of text without realizing it; **confusion of letters of similar form** and **marginal gloss** – insertion into the text something that was written in the margin. Scholars study the manuscripts so as to get rid of these copying errors and edit the original text, so far as it can be done. I should think at least 90% of these errors have been eradicated in the modern printed texts. The remaining uncertainties scarcely affect the modern Bible-reader and most Christians do not bother about the footnotes in our Bibles that tell us about variant readings. Few of them are important.

It is amusing to find that scholars write as if pastors engage in textual criticism! Mostly they do not and I have never heard a sermon (though I have read a few) in which the preacher takes into account variant readings. My favourite preachers and writers treat them as totally unimportant – which most of the time and for all practical purposes is true!

Now that such a lot of textual work has been done the remaining questions are so tiny that they are largely insignificant for the ordinary Christian, and even the preacher hardly needs to bother with many of them. But there are some matters that we should keep in mind.

There is the question of what is called "the majority text". The best manuscripts of the Greek New Testament are undoubtedly the earliest. The later manuscripts have the most corruptions, and it is the late manuscripts which amount to more than 80% of the manuscripts that exist. The remainder that are older, less than 20% of the total, are more reliable. In the fourth century the text was standardised and from that point onwards the vast majority of manuscripts being copied followed the standard text that had been created. This is called the "Majority text" or the "Byzantine text". Also in 1550 the printer Robert Estienne, also known as Stephanus (1503–1559), published an edition of the Greek New Testament. His readings were very similar to the Majority text and his style of textual readings following late manuscripts became known as the Textus Receptus – the "received text". It was also Estienne who in 1551 divided the New Testament chapter into verses.

In the King James or "Authorised Version" of 1611, the New Testament translation is based on Estienne's Textus Receptus. It used only fifteen manuscripts, all of them of late date. But there is a small difficulty here. The Textus Receptus is closely related to the text of the majority of the manuscripts, but it is not quite so accurate as the text that is reconstructed from the earliest manuscripts, printed in the Greek New Testament editions published in modern times. It must be remembered, however, that the differences are so small that many people would not even notice them.

The translators of the KJV of 1611 had little choice. Only a few manuscripts were available to them; they had no opportunity to study the earliest texts. In a typical Greek New Testament published in modern times there are 3,743 verses in the four gospels. In the King James version of 1611 there were 3,779 verses. The difference arises because of the tendency of scribes to insert additions into the text as they were copying manuscripts. In modern printed editions of the Greek New Testament these are a few verses left out because they are not to be found in the best manuscripts coming from earliest times in the transmission of the text. They tend to leave out Matthew 16:3; 17:21; 18:11; 23:14; Mark 7:16; 9:44, 46; 11:26; 15:28; 16:9–20; Luke 17:36; 23:17; John 5:4; 7:53–8:11. Also a few verses (Matthew 5:44; 6:13; 16:2; 20:16, 22, 23; 27:35; Luke 4:4; 9:54–55; 11:2; 23:34; John 5:3) are shorter in modern printed texts for the same reasons; the best texts have slightly shorter wording.

One difference in the majority texts compared to a reconstructed text based on early manuscripts has to do with fasting. The later manuscripts were often produced by scribes in monasteries who took great delight in fasting. As a result they tend to add references to fasting that are not to be found in the early manuscripts. The King James version of Matthew 17:21 says, *"Howbeit this kind goeth not out but by prayer and fasting."* Modern translations follow manuscripts which do not have verse 21 at all. It was inserted from Mark 9:29. But even in Mark 9:29 the best manuscripts have no reference to fasting. *"This kind can come forth by nothing, but by prayer and fasting"* says the KJV. But the modern translations rightly have, *"This kind cannot be driven out by anything but prayer"* or something similar.

In the same way the KJV has in Acts 10:30 the statement of Cornelius, *"Four days ago I was fasting until this hour."* But it is a late reading. The better manuscripts have *"Four days ago, about this hour..."* The reference to fasting was added later and was never in the original text. 1 Corinthians 7:5 (KJV) says, *"Defraud ye not one the other, except it be with consent for a time, that ye may give yourselves to fasting and prayer..."* Again the reference to fasting was not in the original text. Early manuscripts say, *"...and come together again, that Satan tempt you not for your incontinency."*

Other places where there are important variants in our New Testament are Mark 16:9–20 and John 8:1–12 (both late additions to the text). The end to the Lord's prayer ("for yours is the power...") is an addition. The words of the Ethiopian eunuch in Acts 8:37 are omitted by most modern translations for similar reasons. The worst corruption of this kind in the Textus Receptus is 1 John 5:7 and a few words in verse 8. They are not found in any **Greek** manuscript before the fifteenth century! The are first known in fourth century **Latin** manuscripts and seem to come from a Latin Christian writer. Even the New King James version (which generally follows the Majority text and not the earliest manuscripts) leaves it out, quite rightly.

Preachers ought to be aware of textual variations and at a few points the subject is important to them. Occasionally in a passage with a variant reading the preacher ought to know what reading he is following and why. Gordon Fee mentions variant readings in John 1:34 (Son of God or "Chosen One"?) and I myself like to preach on 2 Corinthians 3:1–3 where there is an important variant reading. These examples are considered again below.

My mentor and pastor, Lloyd-Jones, was not very bothered about this subject, but his neglect at this point occasionally led him into a mistake. His sermons on the end of Ephesians 5:30 include some exposition of the phrase "of his flesh and of his bones"[2] but these words should not be in the text! It is a difficult passage he says and "Some have tried to avoid this altogether by pointing out that in certain manuscripts the addition is not present, but it is generally agreed by all the best authorities that in all the best manuscripts this is present."[3] It is encouraging to see a pastor taking note of variant readings. Unfortunately his judgement is quite wrong! Ephesians 5:30b is not in the best manuscripts and it is generally agreed by all the best authorities that the phrasing is **not** original! Lloyd-Jones was following the King James Version of 1611, but it seems that the phrase was inserted from the Greek translation of Genesis 2:23. A scribe filled out the text with an expression that added to the vividness of Paul's words.

On the other hand Lloyd-Jones did mention the extra words that should be found in 1 John 3:1: *"...and so, in fact, we are."* He says, "probably ... it was in the original document." But he is not very excited about it! "It is not, of course, a material point ... just a matter of interest from the standpoint of textual criticism."[4]

I need say no more. The rule is: modern Greek texts produced in Stuttgart or by the United Bible Societies are so accurate they may be taken as virtually the exact words of the original text. This is not **exactly** true, but for the preacher it is as near as makes no difference! These translations give variants in the footnotes, but few of them are important.

This means that one can generally trust the best of the modern translation to have done all the textual work for us. In the New Testament (but not always in the Old Testament) they mention in the margin the cases where there is a significant variant reading. But they will be found to be generally unimportant.

The preacher ought to read a couple of books on textual criticism that say more than I have said, so that he knows what are the basic facts. Occasionally he will have to give some thought to which reading he is following. It will generally be the MT (in the Old Testament) and the standard modern Greek texts (but not the Majority Text) printed by modern Bible societies. If the preacher wants to trust that others have done this work for him – fine! But let him use a modern literalistic translation and keep his eye on the footnotes!

Notes

1. S. Miller, *C.H. Spurgeon and Spiritual Leadership* (Moody, 2003).
2. D.M. Lloyd-Jones, *Life in the Spirit* [Ephesians 5:18–6:9], (Banner of Truth, 1974), pp. 187–191.
3. Lloyd-Jones, *Life* . . . , p. 187.
4. D.M. Lloyd-Jones, *Children of God* [1 John 2:29–3:24], (Crossway, 1993), pp. 13–14.

Text, Interpretation, Translation

I said there were three technicalities involved in our first Bible reading: they are text, basic interpretation and translation. The three are tied together and affect each other. Translation is the last of the three. It is important to note that translation is done **after** the basic meaning is reached. One might think that one could translate the text literally and **then** set about the task of deciding what it means. This would require a **very** literalistic translation for the non-Hebrew-reader and the non-Greek reader. Often this is possible (and this is the value of very literalistic translations) but sometimes it is not! Very frequently the translator must decide what something means **before** he translates it.

Text and interpretation are intertwined

Textual criticism and interpretation are intertwined. The work of deciding which textual variant is correct among many in any given passage of Scripture involves **expounding** each one of them. Fee makes this point in connection with John 1:34.[1] Should it read, *"I have seen ... that this is the Son of God?"* Or should it be, *"I have seen ... that this is the Chosen One?"* There are several reasons for thinking "the Chosen One" is the correct reading. But the reason I am mentioning it is the matter of interpretation. In John's Gospel "Son of God" includes overtones of deity (see John 5:16–30; 10:33). "The Chosen One" is purely Messianic without making any claim of deity. The evidence for each reading is divided. Either a scribe altered a claim to deity to make it a claim to Messiahship-only, or it was the other way round. But basic interpretation points to the latter. In John's Gospel when people confess faith in Jesus the story goes on to mention how someone used an appropriate title for Jesus (John 1:29, 41, 49; 4:42; 6:14; 11:27). Something similar happens here – if the reading is "Chosen One".

Interpretation and textual criticism are intertwined. The point can be emphasized also in connection with 2 Corinthians 3:2. Paul is defending himself. Paul's enemies were saying, "This Paul is an intruder. The headquarters of the Church is in Jerusalem. If Paul really was a true apostle he would have a letter of recommendation from Jerusalem!" So Paul says, *"Or do we need to use (as some people do) letters of commendation to you or from you?"* (3:1b). The Corinthians' own conversion is his letter of recommendation! *"You are our letter, written on **your** hearts, known and read by people everywhere! (3:2) You show that you are the letter from Christ, the result of our ministry, written not with ink but with the Spirit of the living God, not on tablets of stone but on tablets of human hearts"* (3:3). In verse two some Greek manuscripts have "our" (*hemon*); some have "your" (*humon*). This kind of textual decision (which involves the fact that both words sounded the same when being read to copyists) should be made on the basis of the flow of the thought. Paul's illustration makes much better sense if the reading "your" is followed. **The parchment is the hearts of the Corinthians**. The godly character of the Christian is written into his nature by the working of the Holy Spirit. **The readers are people everywhere**. Everyone everywhere read this letter. The world does not read Romans or 1 Corinthians or Philippians. It reads Christians! **Paul was the scribe**. This work of changing lives was achieved by the Holy Spirit, but Paul was like a pen in the hand of God. **Jesus is the author**. Paul does the preaching, but the work is really being done by the Lord Jesus Christ. **The Holy Spirit is the ink**. He is the one who writes the character of the Lord Jesus Christ into our lives. "Who is sufficient for these things?" (2:16b). We are adequate when we are a pen in the hands of the Lord Jesus Christ!

All of this implies that the reading should be "your". The point is: textual criticism does not **precede** interpretation. The two activities affect each other and are interwoven. The preacher cannot entirely sidestep textual criticism. No doubt he leans on the work of others. Preachers cannot spend their time scrutinizing manuscripts. Other people have to do this work for them. But the **preaching** of the Word has to be involved in the final decision. The right reading will always be preachable.

Interpretation and translation are intertwined

Interpretation is, as I say, a task that has to be done before translation. Ephesians 1:11 is a good place to see how this works. Paul is praising God and speaking of God's plan for the future of His people. *"In his good pleasure he is planning an arrangement for the fullness of times. He has a plan to bring together all things in Christ, things in heaven and things in earth – in him. In him also we . . . "* Now we have a decision about interpretation that has to be made. *Eklērōthēmen!* The verb is *klēroō*. It is a simple past (an aorist) tense. It is passive. It has something to do with *klēros* ("lot", "inheritance"). But how should it be taken?

- Is it *"we have obtained an inheritance"* (NASB)? This gives the impression that our heavenly reward in heaven is already secure and fixed. But the New Testament tends to make a distinction between reaching glory and inheritance in glory. The glory is certain (in Paul's thinking) but there is an "if" concerning our inheritance, our **level** of glory.
- Is it *"we have been made an inheritance"*? The idea is biblical. God's people are His inheritance. "Blessed is the nation whose God is the LORD, the people whom he has chosen as **his** inheritance!" (Psalm 33:12). We read of "Israel **his** inheritance" (Psalm 78:71). But this has no parallel in Ephesians and

the passage is speaking of how God has blessed us more than how He Himself is blessed through us.

- Sometimes "we were inherited" is taken to mean "we were chosen". NIV has, *"In him we were also chosen, having been predestined."* But this is oddly repetitive ("chosen . . . predestined").
- There is a better approach, surely. The most likely thought here is: "we were made heirs" (see NIV footnote). I translate: *"we were allocated an inheritance."* That is, the people of God have their good works planned for them (Ephesians 2:10) and are moving towards their inheriting the promises. It is common biblical teaching that believers will "inherit" the promises. They must persist in faith so as to get to their inheritance. Paul often mentions it after he has mentioned justification or sonship (as in Romans 8:16–17) and it seems he does the same here. He mentions the matter explicitly in 1:18. The pathway of our life is also planned. We are allocated an inheritance, "being predestined according to the purpose of him who works all things according to the counsel of his will . . . "

I mention all this only to make it clear that interpretation is a task that has to be done **before** translation.

Contact with the originals

It follows that basic interpretation has to stay as close to the original text as possible. Since most Christians – and even most preachers – do not have a working knowledge of Hebrew, Aramaic (!) and Greek, this has some implications for the Christian preacher. It first of all means that he has to take care that the people he is relying on as his translators are trustworthy, scholarly people, full of wisdom and the Holy Spirit. I think it also means that Christian people have to find ways of staying in touch with the original text despite their lack of skill in the biblical languages. There are at least three ways in which this might be done.

(i) It is important to have some highly literalistic translations at hand. Translations vary in their style. Some are very strict in trying to follow the original word for word. When you read such translations you are virtually reading Greek in English. The English is not very beautiful, and such translations are generally not admired by those who want easy reading! Yet there is something to be said for them. They keep you in touch with the original more than the "easy reading" translations.

(ii) We could learn to read the biblical script – it is not so difficult – and then use "interlinear" Hebrew and Greek Testaments, where the original text is printed with a word for word translation underneath. For beginners in the languages this is a good way of becoming familiar with the original texts.

(iii) Is it so unrealistic to ask more Christians to learn the biblical languages at least in a rough-and-ready manner? You don't have to be able to chat fluently with a guy in Tel Aviv or Athens! The Bible has a small vocabulary compared to what you must know if you are learning (let us say) modern French. The New Testament has about 137,500 words using a vocabulary of just over 5,000 words. But "just over 5,000" is misleading since a lot of them only come once. When you have learned 130 of them, you know a third of the words you will meet in the New Testament! This is surely not so difficult. In these days of computer literacy there are Bible programs where with a few taps on a keyboard a detailed analysis of any word you are reading will appear on your screen. It has never been so easy to read Hebrew, Aramaic and Greek.

Learning the biblical languages goes through four stages. Stage number 1 is where you learn the script. This can done in a few minutes with the Greek and in a day or so with the Hebrew-Aramaic (both of which use the same script). Even this will help you use Greek and Hebrew concordances and follow the discussions of the scholars. You might want to go no further than this – but even this will help!

Stage number 2 is where you work through a textbook teaching Greek. It is rather disappointing because at the end of it you still cannot pick up a Greek New Testament and read it as if you were Paul's best friend. If you start stage 2, you really must go on to stage 3!

Stage number 3 is the really important part. This is where you read a verse a day in Greek (and maybe the same thing in the Old Testament Hebrew) looking up everything you need to look up. With a good computer-program or an Analytical Lexicon (which does all the analysing work for you) it can be done in seconds. As you do this every day of your life, you get steadily quicker in your work, you have to look up less, and you cover more text. This is quite a **dangerous** stage because "a little knowledge is a dangerous thing". You must not make independent judgements based upon your still limited knowledge of Greek. You are not yet an expert (and perhaps never will be) and your knowledge of Greek is to help you be accurate and follow the helps given by the authorities, not to lead you into weird and not-so-wonderful points of interpretation that no one has noticed before! Pastors who do this ("The Greek says . . .") normally reveal their ignorance to any real experts who might be around. You must find what level of knowledge suits you but, in one way or another, stay in touch with the originals!

Paraphrases?

Looser "periphrastic" translations must be understood for what they are. In a paraphrase (J.B. Phillips' *The New Testament in Modern English*, the *Living Bible*, *The Message*) the translator is choosing what he thinks it means and then putting it in easy language for you to enjoy! The advantage of this is that it makes nice reading! The disadvantage is that you are trusting the translator to get the interpretation right! And no interpreter is right all the time! Because his translation is loose it is quite impossible for you to see other possible interpretations. A paraphrase is like a commentary. It is the translator telling you what he thinks it means. But because the translation is **not** literalistic, you yourself cannot see other possible interpretations.

When the NCB paraphrases Daniel 9:24 ("God has ordered four hundred ninety years for your people and your holy city for these reasons: to stop people from turning against God; to put an end to sin; to take away evil; to bring in goodness that continues forever; to bring about the vision and prophecy; and to appoint a most holy place") – it is a fine paraphrase so long as the interpretation is right! But what if he is wrong? A literal translation says nothing about four hundred ninety years. Oddly the New Living Bible (usually periphrastic) is more literal ("a period of seventy sets of seven"). The NCB insists on our taking it one way and will not allow us to see any other possibility. I am not specially critical of this (since all translations have to interpret) – but the more literal the translation the more you can think for yourself, the more periphrastic (a thought-for-thought translation of what the translator **thinks** it means), the less you are allowed to think for yourself. Let's hope your paraphraser is right most of the time! For detailed study use the literalistic translations. Better still, learn a little of the biblical languages!

Word-for-word translations are not popular among professional translators. Of course not! They are concerned with getting their translation across in an easily understandable manner. They want to be unambiguously clear. But what if the original is ambiguous and could be interpreted in more than one way? What then will be "a good translation"? Take the example of 1 Corinthians 7:36 where Paul tells the Corinthians what he advises: *"if anyone thinks he is behaving badly towards his girl."* The Greek word is *parthenon* – "a girl" (with emphasis on chastity and the unmarried state). The ISV translates very literally" *"If a man thinks he is not behaving properly toward his virgin . . . "* (see also KJV. But to whom does this precisely refer to?) There are at least three more detailed interpretations that have been defended.

- The NASB has: *"if any man thinks that he is acting unbecomingly toward his virgin daughter . . . "* (see also ASV).
- The NCB has *"If a man thinks he is not doing the right thing with the girl he is engaged to . . . "* (see also NIV, NLT, NRSV, ESV).

- Another translation might be: *"If a man thinks he is not behaving properly toward his spiritual bride"* for some see a reference here to "spiritual marriages" – couples living together who had resolved not to have any sexual relationship. On this view "his girl" means "his partner in a celibate partership". Moffatt's translation uses the term "spiritual bride". The old NEB went down the same route.

My point here does not concern which interpretation is right but to note that for Christians without Hebrew or Greek it is only the **literalistic** translation (*his virgin* or *his girl*) that allows the matter to be considered. The more interpretive translations in each case obscure the two other possibilities and allow only one view to be seen. For Christians without Hebrew or Greek there is a distinct advantage in the literal word-for-word translations. Since most Christians will not have much skill in the biblical languages only literalistic word-for-word translations enable the different interpretations to be considered by those without the biblical languages.

This thought must lead on to the question: what is the place of paraphrases, such as those by J.B. Phillips, Kenneth Taylor (in the original *Living Bible*), F.F. Bruce, William Barclay, Eugene Peterson? They obscure in a very extreme fashion any possibility of seeing a range of feasible interpretations. They cover up other possibilities of elucidation other than their own. They are in effect **commentaries** on the biblical text, using simple rewording and expansion as a tool to explain how the commentators takes the Scriptures. No one who approves of commentaries can disapprove of paraphrases for the paraphrase is, in effect, a highly compressed commentary. However, the snag is that each paraphrase gives a false **impression** to the unwary, saying in effect **"This** is the meaning and there is no other way of taking it!" – but giving no argumentation. F.F. Bruce's way of doing it was the best. In his *Expanded Paraphrase* of Paul's letters, he had the very literalistic Revised Version printed on one side of the page and his own expanded paraphrase on the other. This is the best way to present the paraphrase for what it really is. Then it

becomes clear that the paraphrase is in fact an *exposition* of the text –
not a translation pure and simple. The layout is saying: "this is a
good translation – and this is my way of taking it." Take Eugene
Peterson's version of the passage just mentioned: *"If a man has a
woman friend to whom he is loyal but never intended to marry, having
decided to serve God as a 'single,' and then changes his mind, deciding he
should marry her, he should go ahead and marry. It's no sin; it's not even a
'step down' from celibacy, as some say."* Taking *parthenon* as "a woman
friend to whom he is loyal" is a fourth interpretation in addition to
the three I mentioned above. If he is right he says it well. But the
other possibilities have disappeared. I am a supporter of good
paraphrases, as long as they are understood for what they are –
commentaries, expositions, one person's view of a possible way of
taking the text. I translate 1 Corinthians 7:36 (fairly literalistically) as
follows: *"If anyone thinks he is behaving badly towards his girl, and she
is mature in years*[31] *and it has to be, he should do as he wants. He is not
sinning. They should marry"* (7:36).

There is another danger in paraphrases. When an interpreter has
a bad and indefensible interpretation, the weakness of the interpretation is disguised by the paraphrase! The paraphrase sounds
quite convincing – but is it **really** an accurate exposition? If it is, well
and good! Paraphrase is a good form of exposition. But paraphrases
also often camouflage an unlikely interpretation! That is why the
literalistic translation and the paraphrase need to be side by side. I
remember that when I was writing my Tyndale Commentary on
Ecclesiastes for Tyndale Press, many years ago, that contributors to
that series were told, "Don't explain the text by using paraphrase!"
I can see why the instruction was given by the publishers (and I
suppose by Professor Donald Wiseman, the general editor). A
paraphrase can disguise a commentator's laziness or incompetence!
However, paraphrases have their uses, when the work has been
done in a high-principled manner.

Notes

1. G.J. Epp & G.D. Fee, *Studies in the Theory and Method of New Testament Textual Criticism* (Eerdmanns, 1993), p. 16.

2. The meaning of "and he/she is *hyperakmos*" is uncertain. Is it "and she is passing the best years of her youth"? Or "and he is strong in his sexual passions"? I think the former is more likely, since the **timing** of marriage seems to be an issue in 1 Corinthians 7, and a reference to age seems to fit with that concern. Whether the man is "oversexed" (as C.K. Barrett has it!) is less of an issue.

CHAPTER 8

Language and Contexts

The secret of interpreting Scripture aright is always to follow the flow of what is being said. There are three great principles here. (i) Keep in mind that the biblical language is basically simple! It is the language of the common people. (ii) Keep every kind of "context" in mind. (iii) Think globally!

Simple language

It might be difficult for modern people to understand, but we ought to know that the biblical books are actually written in very simple language. John's writings (surely the most profound writings ever written) are put to us in almost babyish simple words. He uses such a small vocabulary and such simple words. The apostle Paul is not quite so simple, but even he uses very ordinary vocabulary. Children and slaves were meant to be present when the letter to the Ephesians was read to the Christians in Ephesus. "You children . . . You slaves . . ." says Paul (Ephesians 6:1, 5). He expects them to be present as the letter is read! Philippians is explicitly addressed "To all the saints in Christ Jesus at Philippi, together with the overseers and deacons." The Bible was not addressed to the clergy or the university professors. It was addressed to "all the saints" in each place where a document was sent.

Allow me to use an East African illustration. Suppose I say to you (in Swahili): *utaona cha mtema kuni*. It is quite likely that you will not have the slightest idea what I am saying. And yet a child in a Primary School on the east coast of Africa will have no difficulty in understanding it. In itself it is very simple indeed – and yet you (assuming you are not from East Africa!) might be finding it terribly obscure. How is it that what a child understands on the east coast of Africa you are finding quite difficult?

Now suppose I translate it for you. It means, "You will see what the woodcutter saw." But you **still** don't know what it means! Even when I put it into English you still find it difficult and obscure and are perhaps wondering what I am talking about.

But suppose you have grown up in the Swahili culture of the East African coast. Ah, then it is quite different and quite easy! A Swahili-speaking child understands it. There is a story told among Swahili-speaking peoples. It goes like this. One day a woodcutter went into a deep and dark forest in order to chop wood and bring it back for firewood and for making charcoal. But when he went into the dark interior of the forest he saw something unspeakably gruesome and horrific. He came running out of the forest screaming with fear and terror. But so awful was his experience he went totally insane. From that point on he never spoke anything that made sense – and he never could tell anyone what it was that he had seen in the forest. He was a total lunatic from that day onwards.

Now perhaps you will see what my four babyishly simple Swahili words mean. When a parent or schoolteacher on the East African coast wants to give a fearsome word of warning, he says, "If you are not careful, and you persist in your wickedness, *utaona cha mtema kuni* – you will see what the woodcutter saw!"

Do you understand my illustration? Something that is babyish simple **in itself** can be difficult to follow if you live in a totally different world. This is the kind of difficulty we have with the Bible. In itself it is written in very simple words. Very ordinary people were – and are – meant to be able to understand it. It was addressed originally to very simple people. The Christian Church has not consisted, generally speaking, of intellectuals and clever people.

There were very few intellectuals among the Christians of the first Century when the New Testament was written.

If we find it difficult at times to follow the Bible, there are perhaps two reasons. (i) One is the world of the Bible is rather different from the modern world. This is not much of a problem. As you read and re-read the Bible you soon get to be familiar with its world and its writings make sense as you get to know the biblical world. It is not so difficult, and you can read a few books about biblical times.

(ii) There is a second reason for finding the Bible difficult and this is something quite different. We find it difficult to take in the teaching of the Bible because it is **spiritually** difficult for us. *"The man without the Spirit does not accept the things that come from the Spirit of God, for they are foolishness to him, and he cannot understand them, because they are spiritually discerned"* says the apostle Paul. This has nothing to do with levels of vocabulary. *"The true light that gives light to every man was coming into the world."* This is a very simple sentence. Eleven of its fourteen words are one-syllable words! Yet there are millions of people to whom it means nothing. The difficulty is not linguistic! There are people who do not see light in the eternal Son of God. Jesus said, *"If anyone chooses to do God's will, he will find out whether my teaching comes from God or whether I speak on my own."* But there are people who do not choose to do God's will. They never discover whether Jesus comes from God. But a degree in linguistic or ancient history or even theology will not help them! Until they are willing to do God's will, there will be a blockage in their spiritual knowledge. The easiest paraphrases of the Bible will not give much help. *"How foolish you are, and how slow of heart to believe all that the prophets have spoken!"* said the risen Lord Jesus Christ standing with disciples who were totally unaware of the fact that Jesus was risen from the dead. Their problem was not linguistic.

So I lay it down as a basic principle of interpretation: the Bible is an easy book written for ordinary people. Its language is not jargonistic or clever. Our difficulty might come from the difficulty of crossing into a world of two thousand years ago – but that difficulty is not so great. More problematic is our spiritual stubbornness – but that has to be healed by the new birth. *"The light shines in the darkness, but the darkness has not understood it."* On another occasion, Jesus said to Nicodemas, *"Are you the teacher of Israel, and do not know these things?"* The remedy was the new birth. *"Unless one is born again, he cannot see the kingdom of God."* The fact is: the language of the Bible is very plain and simple. Our difficulties come from elsewhere.

This is, I believe, an important principle of interpretation. The language of the Bible is simple language written for ordinary people. Any interpretation which only is for intellectuals is likely to be wrong! I think of Douglas Moo's interpretation of Romans 7:7–25. He is a great scholar. His commentaries on Romans[1] and James[2] are admirable and for scholarly people his books are among the first that I would be ready to recommend. But – for several reasons – I am not convinced by his interpretation of Romans 7:7–25. His view is that the "I" of Romans 7:13–25 is "Paul himself in solidarity with the Jewish people."[3] His interpretation is obscure and difficult to apply to our own lives in any practical manner. He thinks there is a salvation-historical sequence in verses 7–12[4] and into verses 13–25. It deals, he thinks, with the Jewish people under the Mosaic law.[5] I have many objections to this but I mention only one: can this be preached to ordinary people? If not I am doubting its correctness. For the Bible **was** addressed to ordinary people.

I also think of Karl Barth's interpretation of predestination. Barth – the Swiss theologian who died in 1968 – said that in Jesus everyone was predestined. Jesus is the electing God and Jesus is the man who is chosen. There is no such thing (taught Barth) as a true choosing of some persons but not others. Barth rejected the teaching of the sixteenth-century preachers "departing from it so radically" (as he wrote), and from everyone else's teaching as well! Barth's teaching cannot seriously be said to come from the pages of the New Testament, but there is another matter which I find interesting. Barth's teaching is not able to be preached to ordinary people. I used to wonder what it would be like if the preaching I did had to be done in rural Kenya or India or Zululand. Since that time I have preached in all of those places and have discovered that the most profound Pauline teaching can be preached to the humblest villagers, among people who know no western language and who do not own a single book apart from the Bible.

When one really gets to see by the Holy Spirit what Paul – or Peter or Hebrews or whoever – is saying, one finds it is always preachable. But the interpretations of theological specialists cannot be made simple for ordinary people, and are only enjoyed by a few intellectually trained Westerners and their followers. I can imagine preaching Romans to unlearned villagers – and have done so. But the philosophical versions can never be made comprehensible to the ordinary person.

With the message of Scripture you can get across the teaching sooner or later. You use illustrations and simple vocabulary and you teach "line upon line, precept upon precept" to get Paul's teaching understood. You teach repetitively. However, there is no way one can do the same thing to get across to ordinary people the teaching of Barth or Pannenberg or Moltmann or any of the big names in academic theology. I have had Barth's twelve hefty volumes of "Church Dogmatics" for years and have written essays on Pannenberg and the like. But I have not discovered from their writings much that would ever bring a person to a real knowledge of the living Lord Jesus Christ. Predestination in post-Kantian academic theology reminds me of what Calvin said about Italy. "I went there that I might have the pleasure of leaving it!"

Even with Moo (a much more helpful expositor!) I have a similar difficulty when I read him on Romans 7. I doubt whether the Christian slaves in first century Rome would have had much interest in the salvation-historical sequences of Israel's history. To take it in what Moo calls a "pietist" manner (where personal experience is involved) is much more likely to have been what was on the heart of Christians in first-century Rome. Also in Romans 5–8 Paul's points always have an **individual** application. The blessings of justification, peace with God, hope that is not disillusioning, the love of God for us sinners (one at a time!) those people (a collection of individuals) who personally **receive** the abundance of God's grace – all these matters involve individuals. Continuing in sin (Romans 6:1) is surely something that **individuals** have to avoid. Each person has to let not sin reign in his body. This is not done collectively or only in a salvation-historical manner. When Paul says in Romans 7:5 that "when we were in the flesh, the sinful passions which were aroused by the law were at work in our members to bear fruit to death", is he thinking of something collective and **not** individualistic (and Romans 7:7–25 is surely the exposition of verse 5!)?

Whatever might be the meaning of Romans 7:7–25 (and I will not give a full exposition here, though I say a little more below!) it has to be something where the difficulty is spiritual rather than linguistic, which continues the themes of personal relationship to God that are involved constantly throughout Romans 5–8, **and where the wording is taken in a simple manner**. I would lay this down as a basic principle of interpretation. New Testament vocabulary is simple and un-jargonistic. There are very few technical terms in the New Testament (though our gap in time and space may make them seem technical as we look at them from a linguistic and cultural distance). The preachers keep their Hebrew and Greek grammars nearby and their fingers tap away on computers which flash dictionary definitions on computer screens (maybe!) – but remember that all of their studies are to help them get back to what was written simply to ordinary people. Don't get weird and wonderful in your reading of the Bible languages!

Notes

1. D.J. Moo, *The Epistle to the Romans* (NICNT), Eerdmans, 1996.
2. D.J. Moo, *The Letter of James* (PNTC), Eerdmans, USA; Apollos, UK; 2000.
3. Moo, *Romans*, p. 448.
4. Moo, *Romans*, p. 449.
5. Moo, *Romans*, p. 450.

Watching the Context

The second great principle in Bible interpretation is watching the context. But there are many types of "context" that have to be watched.

History and geography

A sermon of mine on "Challenges to Faith" based on Isaiah 7:1–14 after an introduction talking about faith continues like this:

> Isaiah has to deal with the very great unbelief that was to be found in the two nations, Israel in the north and Judah in the south . . .
>
> The situation was as follows. Assyria in the far north-east was threatening to conquer all the lands at the eastern end of the Mediterranean Sea. To the south was Syria or Aram. Further south was Israel (also called Ephraim). And further south still was Judah, whose capital was Jerusalem. All of the promises of God involved Judah, Jerusalem its capital city and the line of kings who descended from King David.
>
> In Isaiah's time the problem that Judah had to face was,
>
> - whether (i) to become an ally of Assyria,
> - whether (ii) to combine with Syria and Israel in order to resist Assyria,
> - or whether (iii) to do nothing and stay independent altogether and trust God.

Ahaz chose the first option. He became an ally of Assyria. Then Syria and Israel invaded Judah, perhaps to prevent Judah from supporting Assyria in a time of war.

... It is now at least eight years after Isaiah's call. King Jotham (740–732 BC) has come and gone. King Ahaz is ruler of Judah. Syria and [northern] Israel have been allies for many years but now their soldiers are assembling together again, getting ready to invade Judah for a second time. Ahaz hears about it. *"Now the house of David was told, 'Aram has gathered together with Ephraim'; so the hearts of Ahaz and his people were shaken, as the trees of the forest are shaken by the wind."*

Then I have my sermon points which I preach from Isaiah 7:1–14. (1) Faith has to persist despite serious challenges. (2) Persisting in faith sometimes means standing still while God gives a great victory. And so on. But I quote this sermon of mine to make this point. **The history and geography are important**. When we are interpreting the Bible and drawing out its significance, the historical context and the geographical context have to be watched. The message of the need of confident faith when in trouble will not stand out unless the historical-geographical situation is described. What God was saying in **that** situation will help us know what God is saying in **our** situation.

Purposes and occasions

To understand any piece of writing you have to understand where it is coming from, and what was the occasion and purpose of its having been written. All of the writings within the Bible were written for particular occasions. The books of the Law (Genesis to Deuteronomy) were history-books written to record Israel's origins as one of the nations of the world, and the origin of the Law God gave to it. The prophetic books (Joshua-to-Kings, Isaiah-to-Malachi) were written to record the preaching of the prophets as they reminded God's people of their history, so as to call the nation back to loyalty to God and His Law. The musical books of the Bible

(Psalms, Lamentations) enable us to express feelings of emotion, sorrows and joys, with praises and confessions. The wisdom books were written to keep Israel intellectually alert as the people were called to put what they knew into practical godliness. They give the people of God not law but wisdom as they face suffering (Job) and the enigma of life (Ecclesiastes) and the greatness of love-relationships (Song of Songs), and call upon the redeemed to put their minds to work in attending to the finer details of godliness (Proverbs). As the Hebrew Old Testament began with history books, so its ends with history books. The Book of Ruth (late in its position within the Hebrew Old Testament) was written to recall the origins of the family of David and to illustrate what it means to be rescued by a Davidic kinsman-redeemer. Esther reminds us that the people of God may face fearful opposition from forces and powers which want their extermination. Ezra-Nehemiah lets us know that there is work to be done in the kingdom of God. Then the Old Testament ends with 1–2 Chronicles surveying the history of God's kingdom from Adam to the Babylonian exile and pointing to the purposes of God in protecting and guiding His people.

The New Testament books also have fairly obvious themes. The Gospels and Acts are shaped to show that the Lord Jesus Christ is the fulfilment of the purposes of God. Matthew makes the point that Jesus is God's king. Mark presents the basic facts of Jesus' ministry. Luke-Acts begins by expanding Mark's story, and shows how much salvation is by grace, and how it was continued in the Church by the power of the Holy Spirit. John's Gospel highlights the evidence that Jesus is the divine Son of God, the Giver of eternal life. The twenty-one epistles of the New Testament are all pastoral letters written to churches, at least ten years – and generally much more – after the day of Pentecost. They are the work of pastors guiding and protecting the spiritual awakening that began in the power of the Holy Spirit on that day. Then the New Testament ends with a book that surveys the history of God's kingdom from the days of Israel (the woman who gives birth to a child) to the fulfilment of God's plan of salvation (the marriage supper of the Lamb) – the Book of Revelation.

All of these books were written on particular occasions with particular purposes. If we are to understand them we must know their occasion. We must grasp where they are coming from and where they are going to. We interpret them and apply them in the light of what their writers were seeking to say – under the inspiration of the Holy Spirit.

Often it is enough to know only **generally** what is the purpose of any part of the Bible. But sometimes it is necessary to know more precisely what that purpose is. Let me mention two of them where the precise purpose of the writer – Paul – is vitally important. The first of them is 1 Corinthians 7. Consider for example what Paul says in 1 Corinthians 7:39–40. *"A woman is bound to her husband as long as he lives. But if her husband dies, she is free to be married to whom she wishes, only in the Lord.* [40]*Yet in my judgment she is happier if she remains as she is."* Here is a clear word of advice; it is not any kind of strict law. But compare this with what the apostle says in 1 Timothy 5:14. *"So I want the younger widows marry, bear children, manage their households, and give the adversary no occasion for slander."* Here is a clear case where the apostle gives directly opposite advice in two different situations. Clearly something unusual was happening in Corinth (and perhaps in Timothy's Ephesus also). Our understanding of 1 Corinthians 7 must take into account that verse 26 speaks of a "present distress". Clearly there was some crisis taking place in Corinth, perhaps persecution, perhaps a famine. It is not the "crisis" of the Second Coming of Jesus that was in mind, for that would be true at **all** times and would not account for Paul's unusual instructions here. Paul's main point here is: a time of acute distress is not the time to be getting married. So there is a difference between 1 Corinthians 7 (on the one hand) and Ephesians 5:22–33; 1 Timothy 4:3; 5:14 (on the other hand). Among the various things Paul has to say about marriage, 1 Corinthians 7 is **unusual**; the instructions in Ephesians and 1 Timothy are the more normal. It would be a mistake to take 1 Corinthians 7 as "normal" and Ephesians and 1 Timothy as unusual. It is the other way around. Ephesians and 1 Timothy are normal and 1 Corinthians 7 speaks of an unusual, out-of-the-ordinary, situation. We shall go wrong in interpreting and applying 1 Corinthians 7 if we do not take this in account. Historically the Roman Catholic section of Christendom has made much of 1 Corinthians 7, forbidding the Pope and the clergy to get married and pushing singleness as a superior spirituality. Others have done something similar. But the function of 1 Corinthians 7 is not to lay down a law for all time! Are we really to treat verse 29 as standard, permanent advice ("From now on, let those who have wives live as though they had none")?! Clearly there is some great pressure coming upon the Christians in Corinth. It might have been persecution. It could have been a famine. Whatever the distress was it was severe enough for Paul to be saying: this is not the right time to be getting married. Paul is giving somewhat abnormal teaching. He is giving advice about marriage **in a time of special distress**. His advice is different from what he says in Ephesians 5 and 1 Timothy. Clearly there was some exceptionally difficult situation in Corinth and Paul is relating to it. This is a place where the **occasion** of the letter is vital.

Quite probably 1 Timothy is also designed to meet a special occasion. The two letters show clearly that there was a somewhat different crisis there also. There were people teaching false doctrine with "myths and endless genealogies, which promote speculations" (1 Timothy 1:3–4). Timothy was to get the church right again (1:3). Some of the Christians had "wandered away" (1:6) and were "desiring to be teachers" (1:7). Paul wanted the men in the congregation to be models of prayerfulness and calmness (2:8); and he wanted the women to be sensibly dressed (2:9), attentive to good works (2:10), eager to learn more of Christian godliness (2:11). They are not to teach in any way that exercises heavy authority over a man (2:12). They are to follow the pattern of creation in which Adam was the leader in a team of two equals (2:13), and avoid the situation in which a woman steps out of that role and so falls into deception (2:14). Yet at the same time the women are to be quite sure they are of equal status to any Christian man and that the life of godliness will bring them to heavenly reward (2:15).

Some of the men must be appointed as new elders (3:1–8; there had surely been elders before this time). They must have shown skill as heads of homes before becoming heads of churches (3:4). Others must be appointed as new deacons (3:9–10, 12–13). The women associated with them must be faithful women (3:11).

It is clear that a lot of this had to do with a crisis of false teaching. There were "irreverent, silly myths" being taught (4:7). Timothy had a lot of authority and was to give each group in the church appropriate instruction (5:1–6:2a). There were special instructions for widows young and old (5:3–16). Some were "enrolled" with special ministries (5:9). A special problem was that some of the younger ones were using their spare time to do a lot of house-to-house visiting (5:13), becoming "not only idlers, but also gossips and busybodies, saying what they should not" (5:13). Some had "already strayed after Satan" (5:3–15).

It is clear that Paul has reason to speak of individuals arising who teach "a different doctrine and [do] not agree with the sound words of our Lord Jesus Christ and the teaching that accords with godliness" (6:3). It seems that false teaching also brought in some extra money (6:9–10). The first letter emphasizes the severity of the crisis. "Avoid the irreverent babble and contradictions of what is falsely called 'knowledge,' for by professing it some have swerved from the faith" (6:20–21).

When Paul wrote his second letter the problem was still around. Timothy was still having to take great care to "guard the good deposit" of the gospel (2 Timothy 1:14). Many people had turned away from Paul, including some influential men (1:15), even Onesiphorus, who had once been so supportive (1:16–18). Faithful men were needed (2:2). Still the heresies were around. Paul says: Avoid irreverent babble, for it will lead people into more and more ungodliness and their talk will spread like gangrene. Among them are Hymenaeus and Philetus, who have swerved from the truth, saying that the resurrection has already happened. They are upsetting the faith of some (2:16–18). There were still "opponents" (2:25) who had not come to repentance (2:25). It seems that the false teachers were particularly successful among the women. Among Paul's opponents were people "who creep into households and capture weak women, burdened with sins and led astray by various passions" (3:6).

It will be noticed that in reconstructing the situation in Ephesus I have not gone **outside** the New Testament. I have not read into the text any information not to be found in the New Testament itself. This is an important point. Any interpretation which demands information not available to the **original** readers is suspect; and equally any interpretation which demands some kind of information not available to ordinary people **today** is dubious. If the interpretation of the Bible requires highly specialised knowledge then it cannot be a book for ordinary people. Although we need to know the "situation" of each book of the Bible, knowledge of that situation must come from the Bible itself. When additional knowledge is available, from outside of the Bible itself, it is always of interest, and sometimes is very helpful. But we must be careful not to build doctrine on scholarly reconstructions which might be abandoned in a few years. It is the biblical material itself which must be our foundation for evaluation of the situation. If it is not possible to reconstruct the situation **from the biblical material** then we must believe that the information we have is sufficient and we do not need more than we have. But when such information actually is available in the text itself, it will be important in our interpreting the text and even more in our learning how to apply the biblical text to our own world.

Structure and Flow of Thought

Structure

Another vital key to the understanding of Scripture is structure and flow of thought. Modern books have sections and chapters and sub-headings. It has increasingly been realized that ancient documents are much the same. They too have their own ways of marking out sections of what they were writing. They could have headings. For example, Jeremiah 3:6 is a dated internal heading: *"The Lord said also unto me in the days of Josiah the king."* They could have chiastic [X-shaped] headings. For example, in Genesis 2:4 an A-B-B-A structure can be seen. It is a way of marking an internal heading. *"These are the generations of the heavens and of the earth when they were created, in the day that the Lord God made the earth and the heavens."* Translation which put verse 4b at the beginning of a paragraph are making a mistake. A lengthy section can go over the same or similar material twice, as happens in Isaiah 7–11,[1] and in Romans 7:7–25 (considered below), and Zechariah 9–14[2] in clearly marked sections.

I suppose structure is not so important in twenty-one of the story-books of the Bible (**Genesis-Esther, Mark-Acts**) where chronological sequence is observed a lot of the time and this in itself enables the reader to keep his sense of direction.[3]

Some books move through sections which are easy for anyone to see (**Job, Daniel**). **Lamentations'** five poems are clearly marked. **2–3 John** is very simple.

Psalms is a special case since there is the possibility that Psalms as a whole moves forward in an orderly sequence[4] and each psalm also has structure. Alec Motyer's "Psalms" pays special attention to the structure of each psalm,[5] and he has also produced good analyses of **Isaiah**,[6] **Zephaniah**,[7] **Haggai**.[8]

Proverbs might be thought to be specially lacking in structure especially in chapters 10–31, but there is perhaps more to be said.[9] Certainly the poems of Proverbs 1–9 move forward in orderly fashion, and one day someone might be able to show that there is structure even in what seems casually arranged in later chapters. However, we can cope with Proverbs without a clear thread of thought through chapters 10–31. Its main sections are clear.

But in other books the reader gets lost if he or she does not have a sense of direction. In some books it is specially vital to follow the flow of thought. In some of them I myself have tried to produce analyses which will help me to know where I am going as I try to follow the thought of the various inspired books (notably **Ecclesiastes**,[10] **Song of Songs**,[11] **Jeremiah**,[12] **Ezekiel**,[13] **Joel**,[14] **Amos**,[15] **Micah**,[16] **Habakkuk**,[17] **Zechariah**,[18] **Malachi**,[19] **Hebrews**,[20] **1 John**,[21] and **Revelation**.[22]

Hosea's main sections must be noted since they do not tally with the biblical chapters. They could be laid out as follows:

I. THE FAMILY-LIFE OF HOSEA & ITS MESSAGE (1:1–3:5)
A. Introducing Hosea, 1:1
B. Family Tragedy, 1:2–2:1
C. Aggressive Remedies, 2:2–13
D. Promise of Renewal and Restoration, 2:14–23
E. The Recovery of the Marriage, 3:1–5

II. THE MESSAGE OF HOSEA ELABORATED (4:1–14:9)
A. Three Blunders in Israel, 4:1–3
B. A Priest's Family, 4:4–19
C. Unable to Turn to God, 5:1–7
D. Sound an Alarm! 5:8–12
E. A Mistaken Remedy, 5:13–15

F. Returning to the Lord, 6:1–3

G. Love Like the Morning Mist, 6:4–6

H. The Road to Shechem, 6:7–7:2

I. The Burning Oven, 7:3–7

J. Half-Baked Israel, 7:8–16

K. Calves and Kings, 8:1–8

L. Bad Company, Bad Habits, 8:9–14

M. Lost Inheritance, 9:1–9

N. The Beginning and the End, 9:10–17

O. Despising the Goodness of God, 10:1–8

P. Seeking the Lord, 10:9–15

Q. Called from Egypt, 11:1–11

R. Jacob the Deceiver, 11:12–12:13

S. The Last Enemy, 12:14–13:16

T. The Lover's Plea, 14:1–9

If **Hosea** is read with these sections treated as distinct units the reader will not get lost!

In other cases the commentaries provide good sectional analyses (I think of **Obadiah, Jonah, Nahum, Paul's letters, 1 and 2 Peter**).

Matthew requires special attention because it is not at all chronological in chapters 4:17–16:20. At this point the book is moving forward in topics. I have tried to survey the movement of its thought elsewhere.[23] I argue that the other Gospels are much more in chronological sequence than Matthew.

There is an underlying analysis of **James** in my little exposition of it, but I do not state it very explicitly. Motyer spells it out more clearly.[24]

I give attention to **Jude** below.

I believe these analyses are quite important in enabling us to follow the thread of thought, and I myself have done my best in various places to provide analyses that the authors would have agreed with! I would like to think that if I could chat to (let me say) Ezekiel, showing him my analysis of his material, and saying to him, "This is how you laid out what you were saying," he would reply,

"Yes, you have written it out your own way, but that is exactly what I was doing." At least that is the aim of Bible analysis of this kind. It should be more than a list of contents.

Structure – Ecclesiastes – a test case

Let me come back to Ecclesiastes because the interpretation of this book is a good example of how crucial it is to follow structure.

What is the theme of the book? Here is something over which sincere Christian believers have disagreed. A hundred or so years ago many Old Testament scholars reckoned that it was a sceptical book but that "orthodox" verses had been added to make it more orthodox than it really was! Verses like Ecclesiastes 3:17; 5:19; 8:5, 12, 13 and others (for some writers few, for others many) were "orthodox" additions off-setting the scepticism of the basic text. The idea was that the writer was a heretical sceptic, but someone made him more acceptable by inserting statements like, "God will judge the righteous" or "I know that it will be well with those who fear God" or "Whoever keeps a command will know no evil thing" – just so as to make Qoheleth sound more orthodox than he really is. This idea has now been abandoned; few people hold to this approach today. There was never any evidence for it! But the strange thing is that even though the "orthodox" verses are now reckoned to be genuine, the book as a whole is still often treated as though it was very sceptical. When Ecclesiastes was interpreted as a sceptic certain verses had to be got rid of! Now those verses have come back again (so to speak) but Qoheleth is **still** reckoned by many to be a sceptical fellow! One Bible-believing scholar (Tremper Longman) says we learn from Ecclesiastes by treating it as an inspired record of hopelessness! It is a bit like reading in the Bible what the devil says (as in Genesis 3:4, for example). It is there not for us to believe, but for us to take as an inspired account of what not to believe! The orthodox verses still are a bit of an oddity, in this view. It is Qoheleth's saying, "The world is meaningless so we had best just enjoy ourselves" – but we are meant to disagree with him![25]

The best way to find out what Ecclesiastes is all about is simply to get into the text and see what it says! But I believe the flow of thought is vital! My view of Ecclesiastes is that he spends two chapters expounding and explaining what it is like to live life without God (1:2–2:23). Then he presents a partial answer (2:24–26) which he works out in further detail (3:1–22). There cannot be a **complete** answer because even the life of faith is not so rosy in this fallen world. But, says Qoheleth, we can cope if we have faith in a good and sovereign God.

Then on the basis of what he has said he spends a major central block of the book considering various aspects of life on the basis of what he has said about our overall view of life (4:1–10:10).

The last section is a sustained appeal that we should live a life of faith in the Creator-God who is our judge and the Giver of the good life. We do so speedily because life is short (11:1–12:7)! Then the book closes in 12:8–14 not – be it noted – with a criticism of him as a sceptic, but with a recommendation of Qoheleth as a wise and skilful teacher of the things of God.

The flow of thought is a vital matter. If you just dip into Ecclesiastes here and there, you will occasionally hit some very orthodox-sounding verses, and you might happen to hit 2:23 where the pessimism reaches suicidal depths.

The correct approach to the disagreements within Ecclesiastes is surely a structural one. Tremper Longman does not see much structure or development of argument in the book. He tends both in his *Ecclesiastes* and in his *Song of Songs*[26] to see only small units, but he does not see **significant** forward movement in over-arching sections. But I believe if more attention is given to the flow of thought, there is something more profound to be discovered in Ecclesiastes (and Song of Songs also, where Tremper Longman sees twenty-three love poems, but I see six!).

- In the 222 verses of Ecclesiastes the exhortations are concentrated at the end.

- In the first four chapters (making use of the English versification) there are no commands to do anything at all. That the first third of the book is without any exhortation is significant.
- Then in one of the "positive" passages there comes sudden and sustained exhortation. In the section that runs from 5:1–7 there are seven words of command. A change of tone has been introduced into the book.
- From that point on there are imperatives amidst Qoheleth's sections of advice (5:8; 7:9, 13, 16, 21; 8:2, 3).
- Another "positive" passage contains sustained exhortation in 9:7–10.
- Then one the proverbial sections ends with a word of command (10:20) and from that point on there is sustained exhortation again in 11:1–12:8 with 15 verses out of 18 containing exhortations (one of which lasts for seven verses).

I believe this is a hint to us of the movement of thought in the book. The book begins with sheer argument and nothing but argument (chapters 1–3). There is no **advice** in 1:1–2:23, only argumentation. Then it moves into proverbial **advice** without much flow of argument, with occasional exhortations, especially in his positive appeals to go to the house of God (5:1–7), and to enjoy life under the approval of God (9:7–10). All of this leads into a last final appeal which is 80% sheer exhortation – an appeal to live life for God. Longman says close study shows that, "Qoheleth's thought rambles" and shows "lack of order"; it "does not follow a detailed outline". I believe this is the exact opposite of the truth. Close study shows that verses 1:1–2:23 are as orderly as the epistle to the Romans! But the argumentative note changes slightly at the end of chapter 2, and by the end of chapter 3 has ceased. Occasional exhortation then begins and continues until the book ends on a climactic flourish, appealing to us to live in this world a life of faith before the human spirit returns to God.

It certainly starts in a gloomy manner. The starting-point is that the earth is subject to a curse (1:2). The basic statement is found in

1:2. "Utter futility"! Toil becomes fruitless (1:3). The passing of generations cannot change the situation (1:4). Nature is going nowhere and is ultimately boring (1:5–8). History is repetitive in its folly (1:9–11). The king has discovered that life has sadness in it (1:12–13) and is futile, brief and unsubstantial [characterised by *hebel*] (1:14). There are kinks and gaps in our thinking (1:15). The more you know the more you ache (1:16–18).

When one turns to pleasure, it is no better. This also is futile, brief and unsubstantial, characterised by *hebel*, meaning "futility" (2:1–2). The king tells the story of how he found out about the superficiality of pleasure seeking (2:3–10); at the end of his quest the conclusion was the same. Life is futile, brief and unsubstantial, characterised by *hebel* – futility (2:11).

When the king turns to weigh the two possible options: wisdom and pleasure-seeking stupidity he has to admit that wisdom is superior (2:12–13). *"The wise person has his eyes in his head..."* (2:14). But then in another respect it makes no difference because death is an equaliser (2:15–16). *"How the wise person dies just like the fool!"* So life is entirely hateful (2:17) and hope of anything enduring is nil (2:18–19a). This is part of the vanity of life. It is all futile, brief and unsubstantial [characterised by *hebel*] (2:19b). He abandons his quest in despair (2:20) because there is no certainty of enduring achievement (2:21). *"This also is vanity and a great evil"* (2:21). There can be no real gain in life (2:22). Life must be full of terrible weariness and distress (2:23).

Ecclesiastes 2:23 is the lowest point of Ecclesiastes! All the king's studies have brought him to the deepest depth of depression. But surely it can be seen at this point that the thought is not rambling. So far there is no "lack of order". The opposite is the case. Kidner says, "the apparently haphazard structure of Ecclesiastes may conceal a high degree of organisation."[27] Exactly! A definite movement of thought may be seen, and this affects the question of pessimism or orthodoxy in Ecclesiastes.

Personally I doubt if Solomon thought life was meaningless and even a "pseudo-Solomon" ought to have some connection with historical Solomon. It is disappointing, now that the "orthodox" verses are no longer deleted, to find anyone acting as if they were not there. In my judgement a more positive interpretation is required. Wright and Kaiser (and maybe even Eaton) make better sense of the book than Tremper Longman. They give a modern version of the kind of approach found in Matthew Henry, John Cotton, Charles Bridges, Ralph Wardlaw, Hengstenberg, Leupold, and the majority of evangelicals over the centuries. The excellent works in Dutch by G.C. Aalders are similar (in the *Commentar op het Oude Testament* and *Korte Verklaring* series).

But if one sees minimal **structure** in Ecclesiastes and simply picks up a general impression from verse-by-verse study without section-by-section-study, then it is likely we shall pick up an impression of scepticism and not much else. It is this scepticism that has often delighted sceptical people. The evangelical Tremper Longman reckons his understanding of Qoheleth's thought is closest to that of Crenshaw, but Crenshaw himself is rather sceptical![28] He says, "I have been fascinated with the book, perhaps because it makes my own scepticism appear solidly biblical'![29] However, if one takes more seriously the flow-of-thought in the book a different con-clusion will emerge. The problem of futility in the world is first confronted. Then an answer is given – although it is an answer which is far from complete. Upon this basis we are called to live a life of realism, faith and joy. I stress each word – **realism** (for Qoheleth is not suggesting the problem will go away), **faith** without perfect knowledge of what is ahead ("for you do not know which will prosper, this or that, or whether both alike will be good"), and **joy** – for God gives it (2:26; 8:15), maintains it (5:20) and approves of the work of the people who have it (9:7). The structure is the key!

Flow of thought – Jude

The little epistle of Jude gives me another example which will not take up too much space! In Jude verses 4–19, he alternates between argument and description. Around this middle section, verses 1–2 and 24–25 are an opening and a conclusion. In verses 3 and 20–23 he speaks about how he himself feels and he expresses his own repudiation of the trouble-makers in his community. This means that there is a pattern in this letter that scholars often call a palindrome, a structure which runs forwards and backwards through the same topics.

Jude 1–2 are an introduction.
>Jude 3 talks about his own feelings concerning this matter.
>>Jude 4 **describes the trouble-makers**, introducing the theme of the letter.
>>>Jude 5–7 produces arguments from Old Testament parallels.
>>>>Jude 8–10 **describes the trouble-makers**.
>>>>>Jude 11 another argument from the Old Testament.
>>>>>>Jude 12–13 **describes the trouble-makers**.
>>>>>Jude 14–15 another argument from the Old Testament.
>>>>Jude 16 **describes the trouble-makers again**.
>>>Jude 17 an argument from the teaching of Jesus.
>>Jude 18–19 **describes the trouble-makers**.
>Jude 20–23 an argument from himself.
Jude 24–25 Doxology.

Structure in paragraphs – Romans 7 – a test case

The books of the Bible often have large-scale structure but they also often have small-scale structure. Let me give an example. Take Romans chapter 7. You remember how Paul was describing the Law and he says, "We've died to the law; the law cannot help us." And he goes into that famous passage concerning the wretched man, "What shall we say, then? Is the Law sin? No. On the contrary, I would not have experienced sin except through the law" and he goes on, "So the Law is holy; it is spiritual. We know that the Law is spiritual, but I am of the flesh, sold into sin." And he continues, "Oh, wretched man that I am! Who shall deliver me from the body of this death?" People argue about that passage. Is the "wretched man" saved? Is he born again; is he regenerate? Or is he somebody who has not received some holiness-blessing or what? But I would say: the first thing you have to do with that passage is analyse it. Let me see if I can do it with you now.

Romans 7:13–25 goes over the same ground twice. **The structure of the two paragraphs of Romans 7 is clear and should be noted**.

Versa 7a.	Question. Is the Law sin?
Verse 7b.	Answer. May it not be!
Verse 7c.	Counter-proposal: I wouldn't have known what sin was except . . .
Verses 7d–11.	Development
Verse 12.	Conclusion: So then (that's a conclusion): the Law is holy . . .

Then once again:

Versa 13a.	Question. Is the Law sin?
Verse 13b.	Answer. May it not be! Same question, same answer.
Verse 13c.	Counter-proposal. Rather, it was . . .
Verses 14–25a.	Development
Verse 25b.	Conclusion

It is important to see that verses 7–12 and 13–25 go over the same ground twice. He asks the question: Is there something wrong with the Law? Is the Law sinful, wicked, did the devil send the Law? Answer: No! But, instead, he says, what I can tell you is this . . . and he goes on to make a point and develop it. Then he comes to a conclusion. "So then . . . "

Then he goes over the same ground again. He is going over the same ground twice, asking the same question, giving the same answer, working it out, and coming to the same conclusion. The conclusion is: the Law of God will never help you, not because the Law of **God** is wrong, but because **you** are wrong. The only thing the Law will ever do for you is bring you into bondage and despair.

Now, I do not know whether you followed all that. If you have, do you see that the **analysis** has given the meaning? The following of the thread of the argument has unravelled some questions. Many people speak and write – including my much-loved NASB – as if the "wretched man" is spoken of in Romans 7:14 to 25. But do you notice it is not the wretched man of 7:14 to 25; it is the wretched man of 7:13 to 25. Verse 13 is the beginning of a new paragraph.

Romans 7:7–25 is an exposition and development of Romans 7:5. Look at verse 5 carefully and then at Romans 7:7–25 and you will see that Paul simply expands what he said in verse 5. This proves that it is the unconverted man he refers to (because he is "in the flesh" – verse 5). The change of tense in verse 14 does **not** signal a move from past experience to present experience. Actually the paragraph begins in verse 13. The present tense of verse 14 simply puts vividly something that was in a past tense in verse 13. The paragraph (verses 13 onwards) is **not** altogether in the present tense. Again there is no space here for a full exposition[30] but these structural observations are vitally important.

The analogy of the faith

There is another kind of context for our biblical exposition and that is the context of the entire Christian faith. John Calvin, the French reformer of the Church in the sixteenth century saw this very clearly and I can put it in his words. He said to the King of France, "When Paul declared that all prophecy ought to be according to the analogy of faith (Romans 12:6), he laid down the surest rule for determining the meaning of Scripture."[31] To his more lowly readers he said, "My object in this work [of writing Christian doctrine] was to prepare and train students of theology for the study of the Sacred Volume, so that they might both have an easy introduction to it, and be able to proceed in it, with unfaltering step . . . I have endeavoured to give such a summary of religion in all its parts, and have digested it into such an order as may make it not difficult for anyone, who is rightly acquainted with it, to ascertain both what he ought principally to look for in Scripture . . . "[32]

You might expect Calvin to say in his commentaries, "I wrote these expositions of Scripture so that you might know what the total Christian faith is." It would have been correct for him to say it. But he actually said it the other way round: "I wrote this exposition of the total Christian faith." he said, "so that it would help you to read your Bible without making any bad mistakes."

Or let me put it in the words of the twentieth article of the Anglican Church, published in the sixteenth century at which time it was a powerful evangelical denomination. "It is not lawful for the Church to ordain anything that is contrary to God's Word written" it said. In other words, we get our doctrine from the Bible. But then it went on to explain that we read our Bible in the light of the doctrine! "Neither may the Church so expound one place of Scripture in such a way that it contradicts another part."[33]

The point is: you read your Bible in the light of its total teaching. You do not find in it doctrine that is contradicted elsewhere. You find your doctrine in the Bible and you read your Bible in the light of the whole Christian faith.

There is danger in this, of course. You must not read your favourite doctrine into the text of the Bible! You have to read Scripture with an open mind letting it teach you and correct you. You must not force a meaning into it. But still the point of Romans 12:6 stands: "Having gifts that differ according to the grace given to us, let us use them: if prophecy, in proportion to our faith . . . " One thing this means is that we do our prophesying in the light of the entire gospel, and say nothing that contradicts it. The Christian faith is a unity. It holds together. If you think you have found something in the Bible which contradicts the gospel you are making a mistake somewhere. Go back and think again.

Global thinking

All of these different kinds of context will help us follow the meaning of the Scriptures, sentence by sentence, paragraph by paragraph, book by book. But I believe also that our style of thinking is important. When we are trying to follow the Scriptures we use every skill that we have, we pray a lot, but I also believe we are allowed to bring in everything that we know! Bible interpretation is not **narrowly** textual, as if we had our eyes on the text and upon nothing else. We are allowed to bring in spiritual experience and history and everything else we know that will throw light upon the text. Of course these "extra-biblical" lines of approach have to be used carefully. In the end the Bible is its own interpreter, but if we are understand it right our conclusions will not contradict spiritual experience of other bits of information that we have.

Let me give an example of what I call global thinking. Paul himself did this very thing that I am trying to put into words. In Galatians 3:1–5 Paul has given a basic statement of the gospel, but then he confirms and proves his teaching from many different angles. First of all he points to the experience of the Spirit. There had been a time when the Galatians had powerfully experienced the Holy Spirit. It happened not as Paul preached the Law, but as he preached the Lord Jesus Christ. The Galatians' own spiritual experience proves the gospel-message. Have they forgotten what happened to them when they first dramatically came into the experience of salvation? Have they forgotten what happened in the weeks and months that followed? Any Christian who turns to Mosaic legislation for blessing has forgotten the time he received the gift of the Spirit. *"I want to find out from you this one thing. Did you receive the Spirit by works of the law or by hearing with faith?"* (2:2). Paul is obviously referring not to the secret, hidden work of the Spirit bringing us to faith, but to something conscious, something the Galatians will never forget. The Spirit was poured out on the Galatians. The event must have been something like what happened in Acts 10. "While Peter was still saying these things, the

Holy Spirit fell on all who heard the word ... the believers ... were amazed, because the gift of the Holy Spirit was poured out even on the Gentiles ... For they were hearing them speaking in tongues and extolling God" (Acts 10:44–46). Paul's point is: how did this happen? Was Paul expounding the Mosaic Law when suddenly they "received the Spirit"? Was that how it happened? No! Not at all! Paul was preaching the atoning death of the Lord Jesus Christ (just like Peter in Acts 10:43!) when God moved in amazing blessing in their lives. We never **truly** experience the Spirit in any other way. God does not honour legalism by blessing it with the Holy Spirit. Never! So Paul goes on: *"Are you so foolish? Having begun by the Spirit, are you now being perfected by the flesh?"* (3:3).

My point here is this: he is using an argument from experience. What he is saying is not **merely** the interpretation of Old Testament Scripture. He is bringing in something else that everyone who has received the Spirit knows in spiritual experience. Peter did something similar in Acts 2:25–29. Psalm 16 cannot be about the resurrection of David because David's tomb is down the road in Jerusalem. I call this global thinking – bringing in everything you know. It cannot **dictate** what Scripture means, but it can dictate what Scripture does **not** mean.

Let me use a modern example. There are people – Roman Catholics and others – who teach that water baptism is indispensable to salvation. It would be very easy to show from the pages of the New Testament that that is a bad mistake. But there is another way to show that it is nonsense and that is simply to point to the experience of Christians. How can John 3:5 (for example) teach that you have to be water baptized to be saved, when there are hundreds and thousands of people who were indisputably saved before they were water baptized, or indeed even without being water baptized at all. Bring some global thinking into your interpretation! Don't have an interpretation of Scripture which contradicts what is obviously true when you come at the topic from another angle. These hints will have to be enough but I hope will help you learn to think globally!

Notes

1. See J.A. Motyer, *The Prophecy of Isaiah* (IVP, 1993), p. 74.
2. See M.A. Eaton, *Know the Bible* (Hodder & Stoughton, 2002), pp. 421–422.
3. I mention an important digression in Ezra, in Eaton, *Know . . .* , p. 228.
4. See M.A. Eaton, *An Outline of the Psalms* (Chrisco Fellowship).
5. J.A. Motyer, "Psalms", in (ed. D.A. Carson and others, *New Bible Commentary: 21st Century Edition* (IVP, 1994), pp. 485–583.
6. Motyer, *Isaiah*, 1993; also J.A. Motyer, *Isaiah* (TOTC, IVP, 1999), followed by Eaton, *Know . . .* , pp. 60–61, 63, 65–67, 69.
7. J.A. Motyer, "Zephaniah", in (ed.) T.E. Comiskey, *The Minor Prophets* (Baker, 1998), esp. pp. 901–904.
8. J.A. Motyer, "Haggai", in (ed.) T.E. Comiskey, *The Minor Prophets* (Baker, 1998), esp. pp. 968–969.
9. See Bruce K. Waltke, *The Book of Proverbs*, Chapters 1–15 (Eerdmans, 2004), pp. 9–28.
10. M.A. Eaton, *Ecclesiastes* (Tyndale Old Testament Commentaries, IVP, 1983), pp. 48–53.
11. M.A. Eaton, *Know the Bible* (Hodder & Stoughton, 2002).
12. Eaton, *Know . . .* , pp. 114, 117, 119–122.
13. *Know . . .* , pp. 298–305, 307.
14. *Know . . .* , p. 99.
15. *Know . . .* , pp. 346–347. M.A. Eaton, *Joel and Amos*, Preaching Through the Bible (Sovereign World, 1998), pp. 12, 53, 74, 81, 89–90, 105–106, 121, 124–125. It builds on comments in J.A. Motyer's *Amos*.
16. *Know . . .* , p. 374.
17. *Know . . .* , p. 378.
18. *Know . . .* , pp. 419–422.
19. *Know . . .* , p. 426.
20. M.A. Eaton, *God's Last Word, Preaching Through Hebrews 1:1–2:4* (Frontier Publishing, India, 2002), pp. 16–19.
21. M.A. Eaton, *1, 2, 3 John* (Focus on the Bible, Christian Focus, 1996), pp. 25–28.
22. *Know . . .* , pp. 443, 446, 448, 450.
23. See further, M.A. Eaton, *The Jesus of the Gospels* (New Wine Press, 2007).
24. J.A. Motyer, *The Message of James* (IVP, 1985); my comments in M.A. Eaton, *James* (PTTB, Sovereign World, 2004) are not so conspicuous.
25. See Tremper Longman III, *The Book of Ecclesiastes* (NICOT, Eerdmans, 1998).
26. See Tremper Longman III, *The Song of Songs* (NICOT, Eerdmans, 2001).
27. F.D. Kidner, *Wisdom to Live By* (IVP, 1985), p. 108.
28. Longman, *Ecclesiastes*, p. 36.
29. See J.L. Crenshaw, *Ecclesiastes* (OTL, SCM, 1988), p. 53.

30. See M.A. Eaton, *Living Under Grace: Preaching Through Romans 6:1–7:25* (Word, 1994), for the development of these points. My two volumed *Romans* (PTTB) and my larger *Romans* might one day be published.

31. Prefatory address, in J. Calvin, *Institutes of the Christian Religion* (*Institutio Christianae Religionis*), electronic edition (Logos Research Systems, Inc.: Oak Harbor, WA), Beveridge translation, originally published by Calvin Translation Society, 1845–1846.

32. Epistle to the reader, in Calvin, *Institutes*.

33. ... *nec unum scripturae locum sic exponere potest, ut alteri contradicat* ...

III. Getting the Message

"Expository Thoughts"

My subject is prophetic preaching. Everything I have said in section II of this little book is only necessary preliminary. These technicalities ought to be familiar to those of us who are called to minister to the Church of Jesus Christ in this way. But that is all they are – preliminary technicalities. It is not the real heart of our work. We are now approaching the heart of the work of the "prophetic preacher". It is his work of expository meditation; it is his rumination on the significance of the text; it is his "expository thoughts", as Bishop John Charles Ryle put it in his seven books of *Expository Thoughts on the Gospels* (whose chapters are a great example of what I have in mind).

Meditation on the exposition of Scripture is the vital part of Bible reading. It is more vital than stage 1 – the study of technicalities. The tragedy of much modern Bible reading is that it tends to be interested only in technicalities and gathering information and knowledge.

Much more important is stage 2! The Word of God will only have an impact upon the lives of practical men and women if stage 1 (technical information) is carried forward into stage 2 (hearing the voice of God). The more important aspect of Bible reading (although almost totally neglected by modern scholarly commentators!) is the gathering of theological and spiritual "lessons" or "points" or "applications" of the Word of God. The Puritans used to talk about the "uses" of any passage of the Bible they were explaining. The Church of Jesus Christ badly needs to recapture the habit of writing **expository** commentaries of this kind. It is preachers and expositors who ought to do this work. The ideal commentary needs to continue where most scholarly commentaries stop! Even commentary series that contain the word "exposition" or "expositor's" seem to have strangely little **exposition**. Some of them are quite hostile to exposition and tell us you must **only** acquire commentaries with exegesis (basic interpretation). Buy one of these books that gives lists of necessary books for pastors – and you are not likely to find any mention of Bishop Ryle or Charles Spurgeon or A.W. Pink. We are encouraged to interpret Scripture, but **not** to dwell upon its implications. Not surprisingly this produces a generation of Christians who have a superficial knowledge of their people and who can enjoy preachers who dash through Romans in a couple of sessions – but in other respects are tossed around with every wind and wave of doctrine.

I think in this connection of something that Professor F.F. Bruce once[1] mentioned in connection with Karl Barth's second edition of his famous commentary, *Romans*. Barth complained of the tendency of many biblical commentators to confine themselves to a form of textual interpretation which in his eyes was "no commentary at all, but merely the first step towards a commentary." Barth thought Calvin's *Romans* was a real commentary noting "how energetically Calvin, having first established what stands in the text, sets himself to re-think the whole material and to wrestle with it, till the walls which separate the sixteenth century from the first become transparent! Paul speaks, and the man of the sixteenth century hears." Bruce himself confessed, "by Barth's criterion, my volume on the Greek text was but 'the first step towards a commentary'" but went on to say "a man who does not take the first step will never take a second." To this I might add my own comment: Bruce never ever took the second step! He wrote commentaries on at least seventeen books of the New Testament, but none of them can be called commentaries which take "the second step". They all deal with the bare bones of interpretation; they never make the walls which separate the twenty-first century from the first become transparent! Bruce was a historian and his commentaries were never very theological; they never drew out much of the message of Scripture.

The best way I can show what I mean by **expository meditation** on Scripture is perhaps to share some of my own meditations on particular verses of Scripture. Let me put three of them here, one from Romans, one from Hebrews, one from Lamentations. I take them from some as yet unpublished notes of mine.

An expository meditation: Romans 14:14a

I once wrote out an expository meditation (one of four hundred) on half a verse in Romans – Romans 14:14a (*"I know and am persuaded in the Lord Jesus that nothing is unclean in itself."* It went like this. First there is a paragraph in which I state what the basic text is all about.

> **Nothing is unclean in itself** (Romans 14:14a)! Paul comes to the main point that has to be understood. *"I know and am persuaded in the Lord Jesus that nothing is unclean in itself"* (14:10a).
>
> Why does Paul begin with *"I know . . . "*? It is because he has been so slow in getting to this point that the strong will be saying, "Does Paul not realize that nothing is unclean in itself?" Paul says, "Yes, I realize that. I know!" Paul has taken his time in getting to the point because he is concerned about attitudes as well as doctrine. But he does know what the strong are waiting for him to say.
>
> Paul has been *"persuaded in the Lord Jesus"*. There are different kinds of revelations. God has different ways of speaking. Sometimes Paul might be given a vision (as in Acts 16:9; see also Acts 18:9; 2 Timothy 4:17). Sometimes he might be given a fresh and new revelation (see Romans 11:25–26). A mystery is revealed to him. But sometimes revelation might come to Paul through heightened, inspired reasoning. This is what happened in connection with the teaching here. *"I know and am persuaded in the Lord Jesus . . . "* *"Nothing is unclean in itself"* is an inspired revelation. It is part of the Word of God. Yet Paul came to it not by a vision or a message

from an angle. He came to it by "being persuaded", by thinking the matter through under the illumination of the Holy Spirit.

But I do not stop there. I want to **expound** the text. I want to draw out its significance. So I go on with some more thoughts on the matter – like this.

1. **There are philosophies and religions which regard some "things" as unclean in themselves.** Ancient Greek philosophy tended to regard anything connected with matter as wicked or inferior in itself. Anything that gave physical pleasure was treated with suspicion. So Christians who were influenced by Greek philosophy (as many early Christians were) tended to be "ascetic". That is, they severely deprived themselves of any pleasure that had anything physical in it. Colossians 2, for example, refers to people who made restrictive regulations about what you could eat and drink (2:16) and rules about things you could not handle or taste or touch (2:21) and harsh treatment of the body (2:23).

Often in Paul's time these philosophical ideas got mixed up with regulations that were to be found in the Law of Moses which forbade certain foods as "unclean". Of course in the Old Testament it did not mean that they were unclean in themselves. They were simply "unclean" as a matter of ritual or ceremony. They were *symbolically* unclean, *ceremonially* unclean.

2. **Paul insists that there is no material "thing" that is unclean in itself.** There were things in the ancient Law of Moses which were "sacred". They were special to God. They were called "holy", but this kind of holiness is only a matter of being set apart for special religious purposes. It does not mean that the actual thing is some-how holy in itself. A "thing" does not decide to obey God or decide not to obey God. There is no morality or immorality in the thing itself. Matter is not wicked in and of itself (although many of the Greek philosophers held that opinion).

The food laws of the Old Testament were only symbolical. There was no difference between a clean and unclean food in itself. It was simply a matter of symbolism. Unclean foods symbolised non-Israelites; clean foods symbolised Israel (as is made clear in Acts

10:9–23 where eating unclean foods symbolizes fellowship with Gentiles).

3. **Modern Christians need to understand this as well as first-century Christians**. We must try to apply this principle to ourselves. There are certain matters in modern life where one tends to think that the "thing" itself is unclean. There are Christians who will not eat pork and Christians who think tea or coffee is sinful. There are Christians who think it is always sinful to drink wine. Then there are those who think that certain "things" are worldly. It may be a cinema film or a credit card. It might be a novel or a TV programme.

But the fact of the matter is it is not the "thing" that is sinful or holy – but what you do with the thing. There can be cinema films that promote violence or immorality. There can be cinema films that are informative or even that tell the story of Jesus. It is not the "thing" that is wicked or holy; it is what the person does with it. A credit card can be used for spending money on something wicked. A credit card can be used for buying a Bible and paying next week. People who think that the credit card is the sign of the beast of the book of Revelation (and there are such people) are mistaken – and are weaker brothers thinking some "thing" is in itself sinful.

Jesus put it like this. "Nothing that enters a man from the outside can make him unclean" (Mark 7:18). In the days of Jesus the Pharisees regarded unwashed hands as sinful in themselves (Mark 7:2), and they were very strict about clean and unclean foods. Jesus said what really matters is the heart. Sin and righteousness consist of what is taking place in the heart. The trouble with men and women is that we are born with sin in the "heart" – the central core of the human personality. Out of the heart come all the inclinations to sin and malice and impurity (Mark 7:20–22). These arise within man's life. It is not failure to wash the hands that defiles man. It is not some food or some "thing". It is failure to control the wickedness of the heart that constitutes sin.

The principle is: A "thing" is not sinful just because it is a thing. God made everything good (Genesis 1:31). Everything created by God is in itself good and is to be received with thanksgiving and used wisely. To the pure every "thing" is pure (see 1 Timothy 4:3–4; Titus 1:15). No thing is unclean in itself.

This kind of "expository meditation" – or whatever one might want to call it – is what is conspicuously lacking in modern commentaries. The preacher will have to do this for himself! Few books will give him much help.

Notes

1. F.F. Bruce, *Acts*, NICNT, 2nd edition, reprinted 1981, pp. 8–9.

An Exposition: Hebrews 4:16

But let me give a second example. I once was meditating my way through Hebrews, writing up my expository thoughts as I went along. At one step on the way I was thinking about Hebrews 4:16. I did all my commentary reading on the verse; I did my homework on the various interpretations. But that is only stage one. It is stage 2 that interests me. Here is my first meditation.

"Let us then draw near to the throne of grace with boldness, in order that we may receive mercy and that we may find grace to help us at the right time when we are in need" (4:16). I believe in what I call "ordinary praying"! It seems to me that at the moment there is a lot of sensationalist praying, and a lot of what I call special-techniques praying. In recent years people have developed all sorts of tricks and gimmicks with regard to prayer. In their origins I'm sure the new ideas came from God – but often something which originally came from God ends up as a gimmick. I have in mind things like prayer-tourism (as I call it), where you have to go to Timbuctoo in order to pray for Timbuctoo! Or prayer-marches (I'm not precisely against them!) Or twenty-four hour prayer-chains. Or praying through the gates of Jerusalem! Or thinking evangelism takes place by sending intercessors (did Paul send intercessors ahead of him to Philippi – Acts 16?). Sometimes "intercessors" seem to think they are a kind a "Super-Church-Official" whose job is to tell preachers what to do.

But what happened to ordinary praying? Of course public prayer meetings need to be bold and joyful, confident and lively. But I shouldn't want to forget ordinary praying! What happened to the old habit of going into a room or place where there are no people around, closing the door (literally or metaphorically!) and praying to our Father who sees what is done in secret? I suspect we all need to do a lot more "ordinary" praying!

What makes us do a lot of praying? We shall pray much more when we see our need of it. We shall pray much more when we see how much trouble we are in if we don't. And we shall pray much more when we see the sympathy and humanity of our High Priest in heaven! "We have a great High Priest who has passed through the heavens, Jesus the Son of God . . . Let us then draw near to the throne of grace with boldness, in order that we may receive mercy and that we may find grace to help us at the right time when we are in need" (4:16).

There are, it seems, five items for me to think about. (i) What we do – we draw near. (ii) Where we go – to the throne of grace. (iii) How we do it – with boldness. (iv) What we want – mercy, grace. (v) When we get it – in the time of need.

What do we do? We draw near. God wants us to get close to Him. The kingdom of heaven is near – in more than one way. Jesus would sometimes stop and order someone to be brought near to Him. When he came **near**, Jesus would bless him (see Luke 18:40–42). Sometimes Jesus comes near to us. On one occasion when two disciples were very depressed, talking about everything that had happened to them, "Jesus himself came near and began walking with them." It is something Jesus liked to do! (see Luke 24:15). In Christ Jesus, you who were far away from God are brought near through the blood of Christ's death (Ephesians 2:13).

But God likes it when we act first. He likes us to take the initiative. Come near to God, He says, and God will come near to you (James 4:8). It is a surprising thing that we can get near to God at all. He lives in light so bright no one can go near it! (1 Timothy 6:16). He is a consuming fire, and yet we are told to draw near! A better hope has been given to us, and with this hope we can come **near** to God (Hebrews 7:19). "Since we have a great priest over God's house, let us come near to God" (Hebrews 10:21–22). Come to God! Say to Him (in the words of Psalm 63):

God, you are my God.
I search for you.

I thirst for you
like someone in a dry, empty land
where there is no water.
I have seen you in the Temple
and have seen your strength and glory.
Because your love is better than life,
I will praise you.
I will praise you as long as I live.
I will lift up my hands in prayer to your name.

Where do we go? To the throne of grace. *"Let us then draw near to the throne of grace..."* One day everyone will appear before a throne of judgement. We shall see everyone "great and small, standing before the throne" (Revelation 20:12). That will be a throne of judgement. But at the moment we have the privilege of coming to a throne of grace. God is a mighty King. We think of Him (in picture language) as seated upon a throne. It means that He rules over our lives, over our circumstances, over our friends and over our enemies. When we get close to God we are coming to the greatest King in the universe. When He answers our prayer, it is not one beggar giving to another beggar! He answers our prayers as a King being kindly to His friends.

If we are to "draw near" to the throne, it implies that we are often far away from it! If you receive a message saying, "Come to Mumbai" or "Come to Britain", it implies that you are elsewhere at the moment. By nature men and women are **not** near to the throne of grace. They know little of God's sovereignty. They know little of God's grace. Even Christians can forget the graciousness of God, and His great power to control every tiny detail of our lives.

God's throne is a throne of grace. We shall discover He is more gracious than we ever realized. I may be deeply ashamed of myself, but I draw near to God! I may have nothing else to rely on, so I rely on God's gracious kingship! The woman of Mark 5:25–35 had tried everything else for twelve years and found no answer to her need. But one touch from Jesus and all was well! I am specially welcome to God when all else has failed. I come ready to ask for big things. If I ask anything of the Father, within the will of the Lord Jesus Christ,

He will give it me in Jesus' name. What I have asked for before amounts to nothing! Ask, and you shall receive, that your joy may be made full (see John 16:23–24).

That was enough for one day. But the next day I was still wanting to ponder Hebrews 4:16 and I had not finished! Here is my second meditation.

"Let us then draw near to the throne of grace with boldness, in order that we may receive mercy and that we may find grace to help us at the right time when we are in need" (4:16). Where do we go? To the throne of grace. How do we do it? With boldness. The word used here (*parrhesia*) means openness, candour, the confidence to speak boldly, openness to truth, frankness, confident and joyful freedom, freedom of speech. I am to speak to God with boldness. It means there is no waiting in timidity. I can come to the Father at any time through Jesus. There is no forbidden time when the door is locked. I can speak freely, without the kind of restraint that comes from fear of rejection. I can talk to God as a friend. True, I must not speak to Him as if we were an equal! Yet I may talk to Him in childlike simplicity. I may be straightforward with Him. There is no need to try to impress Him. I do not have to use special religious language or endless repetition. I do not have to work up emotion (although of course emotion is not sin and we Christians are often deeply moved as we pray). We do not have to shout as we pray, nor do we have to use a religious whisper. We come with open frankness. We hide nothing. We are not even thinking about how we are praying; we are simply praying! Jesus is sympathy enthroned. We come to Him with great confidence. We are not afraid to argue our case with God and give Him the reasons for what we want.

What do we want? Mercy and grace. When I come to God through Jesus, what is it that I want? My first need is mercy! I do not come to give God anything or to feel strong. I have often sinned. I am unworthy. If God were to deal with me in strict justice I would be in great trouble. God's "mercy" is God's willingness to hold back just punishment or just rejection. Every person in this world is born condemned; we come from a sinful race and we add to its sins ourselves. But even when we experience God's salvation how much we wander, how often we fall! But God is willing to show us mercy – if we come for it at the throne of grace! We need mercy, and we can come being sure that we shall find it! Our need is not greater than God's mercy. Our sins may be piled up high but God's mercy is greater. "Let Israel hope in Yahweh, for with Yahweh there is mercy, and with him *is* plenteous redemption" (Psalm 130:7). God never refused mercy to anyone who came for it.

When I come to God through Jesus, I come for grace to help us. Grace is God's help to those who do not deserve His help. What is it like to be given God's grace to help us? It is when He gives us His presence, perhaps in a very special way. "Do not fear," God will say, "for I am with you. Do not look around in desperation, for I am your God. I will strengthen you and help you; I will uphold you with my righteous right hand" (Isaiah 41:10). Sometimes God helps me by changing the circumstances or by bringing unexpected changes in the events taking place. Sometimes He will give me His presence. Sometimes I shall discover that I am stronger than I ever thought I could be.

When we do get what we need? In the time of need. It may be just in the nick of time! God's special help tends to come "at the right time when we are in need". We may and should pray even before any special need comes along. You never know what might happen at any moment. We are of course always needy people. Living as we should is always beyond our strength. But there are times of special temptation, times when God does not seem so close, times when particular troubles come upon us, times when special callings and special challenges come before us. Whatever the need God's grace is there for us. As our days are so shall our strength be. God's grace will always come to us on time. God is never too early, never too late.

So I must come to the throne of grace – often. I make sure to be there every day. I must knock at God's door frequently, expect mercy, expect to be given help. I must be confident about it. I must say, "As for me, I will call upon God. And Yahweh **will** save me" (Psalm 55:16). We have a High Priest who is utterly sympathetic towards us. He is there for us. We have Him! He lived in this world but He does not forget us now that He has passed into the heaven of heavens, where He reigns with the Father. Like the high priest of the Old Testament He has us on His heart and carries us on His shoulder. Maybe I am depressed by my slowness to grow as I want to. But I may go to Him! I am not to be afraid to draw near to Him. Jesus will listen to me. He is able to understand. Even if what I do is unspeakably terrible I will never find a better sympathizer than Jesus! He has a tender heart. He is a great High Priest! It is His work to hear all the trembling requests of those who feel so unworthy. He will listen to all the complaints of the oppressed, all the troubles of the poor, all the entanglements of those who have fallen into sin. He is appointed by God the Father to take all our troubles to the Father. So let me draw near to God in total confidence that I shall be received, I shall be shown mercy, and I shall be given grace.

This is what I do every day of my life! It is not always written out as neatly as this! Sometimes it is just some scribbled points, maybe in a café in Nairobi! But I cannot be a prophetic preacher unless I hear from God in this way and get clear in my mind what God is showing to me. This is the kind of expository meditation that I do every day! I do not see how anyone can be much of a preacher unless he or she hears from God in this way. And of course this is not just for preachers! This is how every Christian should read his or her Bible. But surely we who are preachers should be leading the way and showing everyone else how to do it!

An Exposition: Lamentations 2:1–6

CHAPTER 13

Here is one more meditation of mine – chosen totally at random. It happens to come from some expository thoughts of mine on Lamentations 2:1–6 (with some technical bits in footnotes).

There has already been some mention of the anger of God – in the first poem. Now a second poem takes up the matter with greater intensity. Once again the poem is an alphabetic one; most of its twenty-two verses have three lines and the first line corresponds to a letter of the Hebrew alphabet. Again J.P. Wiles has a translation which catches the successive letters of the Hebrew alphabet, and expresses it in the sequence of the English alphabet.

> **A** cloud of anger darkens Zion's sky:
> God lays in dust her pinnacles of pride.
> And spurns the footstool of His majesty.
> **B**illows of fire o'er Judah's homesteads flame;
> Relentless whirlwinds wreck her palaces;
> Her nobles pine in slavery and shame.
> **C**onsumed is Salem's strength, her hope expires;
> The hand that once her every foe repelled
> Now circles her with sin-avenging fires.
> **D**eath-dealing shafts from God's own quiver . . .

A constant theme in the first six verses (to look no further) is the anger of God. It is mentioned explicitly six times in six verses (*"his anger . . . the day of his anger . . . his wrath . . . fierce anger . . . his wrath . . . his fierce anger . . . "* (2:1a, 1c, 2b, 3a, 4c, 6c).

1. **The God of the Bible has feelings and emotions**. The picture of
God that we have in the second poem prevents us from thinking
of God as some cold or uninvolved being with no interest in the
concerns of the human race. God is full of passionate feelings about
what is happening on planet earth, especially in connection with His
people. He is no "unmoved mover" (as Aristotle the third-century BC
philosopher would have put it). He is not merely an impersonal
"ground of our being" (as Paul Tillich, the German-American
philosophical "theologian" said). Philosophers tend to imagine a
God who is abstract and coldly unemotional. But the French
mathematician Blaise Pascal (1623–1662) put it better: "The God of
Abraham, Isaac and Jacob – not the god of the philosophers!"
Consider the description of God in Lamentations 2.

> "Ah, how the Lord in his anger has covered Daughter Zion with
>   a cloud!
> He has thrown down the beauty of Israel from heaven to earth;
> he has not remembered his footstool in the day of his anger (2:1).
> Without pity the Lord has swallowed up all the country
>   dwelling-places of Jacob;
> in his wrath he has torn down the fortified cities of Daughter
>   Judah.
> He has brought her kingdom and its princes down to the ground
>   in dishonour (2:2).
> In fierce anger he has cut off every strong horn of Israel.
> He has withdrawn his right hand at the approach of the enemy.
> He has burned in Jacob like a flaming fire that consumes
>   everything around it" (2:3).

We have no cold passionless unmoved Mover here!

2. **The God of the Bible is utterly and totally sovereign**. In
everything said here we see the lordship and sovereignty of God
over the nations. The fall of Jerusalem was not some kind of tragic
accident. It was closely supervised and brought about by the Lord
Himself. God is the king of history. Constantly everything is said to
be done by God Himself. "Yours, O Yahweh, is the greatness and the
power and the glory and the majesty and the splendour, for
everything in heaven and earth is yours" (1 Chronicles 29:11). God

can do anything which is in accord with His character. He can put His people in obscurity and darkness (2:1a). He can pull them down from their status in the heavenly realms (2:1b). He can refuse to keep us in His mind (2:1c). God is sovereign! His kingly power rules over all (Psalm 103:19).

God can withhold mercy! *"Without pity the Lord has swallowed up all the dwellings of Jacob..."* Think of the way in which the sun shines. The sun does not **choose** to shine. It shines unthinkingly and without having any choice. But the God of the Bible is not like anything impersonal! He **chooses** to show mercy. "I will have mercy on whom I will have mercy, and I will have compassion on whom I will have compassion" (Exodus 33:19). And there can come times where, for His own reasons, He withholds mercy.

3. **The God of the Bible is passionately involved in rejecting and hating sin**. There is great mystery here. We do not know why God tolerates sin and evil for even a second! He endures sin and wickedness in this world "with much longsuffering" (Romans 9:22). He can withhold mercy (2:2a) because He is determined to do something about sin in His people. He can take away the strongholds or cities in which we place our hope of security (2:2b). Even the very kingdom which He founded He can bring to an end if it no longer pleases Him (2:2c). Anything which made us strong He can remove. "Every kind of strength within Israel vanishes beneath his fury" – as we might translate 2:3a ("horns" is a way of speaking of "strength"). He can hand us over to enemies (2:3b). He hates sin so much that He will exterminate it; the fire of His holiness destroys that which opposes Him (2:3c).

Lamentations 2:4–6 concentrates on the way God can become an enemy to His people. Just as He fights for them, He can fight against them.

> *"Like an enemy he has bent his bow; his right hand is ready.*
> *Like a foe he has slain all who were pleasing to the eye;*
> *he has poured out his wrath like fire on the tent of Daughter Zion (2:4).*
> *The Lord is like an enemy; he has swallowed up Israel.*
> *He has swallowed up all her palaces and destroyed his fortified cities.*
> *He has multiplied mourning and lamentation for Daughter Judah (2:5).*

Like something in a garden,[1] *he has violently shaken his dwelling;*
    he has destroyed his place of meeting.
Yahweh has made Zion forget festival and sabbath;
in his fierce anger he has rejected both king and priest" (2:6).

But how must we understand this enmity? **The anger of God
against His people is temporary**. It is intense but against His people
it is not everlasting. Lamentations 2:6 is not the end of the poems!
If verse 3 says, "He has burned in Jacob like a flaming fire that
consumes everything," Lamentations 3: 22 says, "Because of
Yahweh's great love we are not consumed." If Lamentations 2:2
says that God can withhold mercy, Lamentations 3:22–23 says "His
compassions never fail" and are "new every morning". This is surely
proof (and the eventual return of Judah to Jerusalem under Ezra and
Nehemiah is another proof) that God's anger against His people is
temporary.

**It was this very anger of God that led to the atoning death of
the Lord Jesus Christ**. No one will ever even begin to understand
the cross of Christ until we see that what took place was Christ's
bearing the anger of God against sin. The death of Jesus Christ was
substitutionary. That is, Jesus died in our place. He died, the
righteous for the unrighteous. "Christ died for us" (Romans 5:8).
There is a penalty for sin. The lamentation over the fall of Jerusalem
gives just a pale shadow of it. In fact the entire human race is under
just as bad a threat. The wages of sin includes everything mentioned
in the poems of Lamentations. But Jesus Christ the God-man took
the punishment upon Himself. In the death of Christ our sins have
been punished by God. Our task is to take hold of the fact in faith –
and feel our conscience to be satisfied and cleansed in the knowledge
that Jesus has died for us. As Martin Luther put it, "By a wonderful
exchange our sins are no longer ours but Christ's; and the righteousness of Christ is not Christ's but ours."[2] The anger of God
against sin has been extinguished by the blood of Christ, for those
who put their faith in God's Saviour. True, the anger of God can
burst out against us again! If we sin wilfully after we come to a
knowledge of the truth there must and will be fiery judgement
against us. The fall of Jerusalem is a sample of what can happen. It
can **seem** as if the anger of God will go on forever. But it will **not** go

on for ever. Because of the blood of Christ the anger of God can never be eternal for His people. The gates of Satan's kingdom of death will not prevail against the Church. And equally the gates of God's anger will never continue eternally against God's elect. God's Israel (and the word "Israel" may be taken in more than one way) will never totally lose the love of God upon them. Lamentations 2 is followed by Lamentations 3! Because of Yahweh's great love we are not consumed.

Some tips for expositors!

Here is my suggestion for the preacher. Work your way through books of the Bible in this way. Don't be preparing sermons! Expound the Word of God for yourself. But here is my tip. **Put your notes into numbered points!** You are not preparing sermons, but later on when you **are** preparing a message you will come back to these notes of yours. You will often find the numbered points are the very things you want to say in your messages to the church. Work through whole books of the Bible. It will take you all your life to do it. If you finish the whole Bible, then you can start again. Read a few expositions that are good models of this kind of prayerful meditation. There are not many of them but here are a few.

- Read Bishop Ryle's seven books of *Expository Thoughts on the Gospels*. You will see what exposition means and the way the good bishop read and **expounded** the Word of God.
- Read the expositions of John Stott (on the Sermon on the Mount, Acts, Romans, Ephesians, 1–2 Thessalonians, 1, 2 Timothy, Titus). They are not detailed and minute – but they will start you off on a life of expounding Scripture.
- Read the expositions of Dr Martyn Lloyd-Jones. They will teach you how to preach. Try the short ones first (his books on Psalm 1, Psalm 51, Psalm 73, Psalm 105, Habakkuk, Sermon on the Mount, John 17, Philippians, 2 Peter), then try the evangelistic sermons on Acts (*Authentic Christianity*, six books).

Then you can get into the big ones reading a chapter per day of Dr Martyn Lloyd-Jones on Ephesians (8 books!) and Romans (14 books!) You will learn a lot.

- Read the books by Alec Motyer (Exodus, Amos, Philippians, James). They are sometimes a bit too compressed. Read them slowly. Chew over them.

- Try R.T. Kendal's two books on James: *Justification By Works* and *The Way of Wisdom*.

- You might even try the *Preaching Through the Bible* series by Michael Eaton! Whatever you think of them, you will have to admit they are **exposition**.

Notes

1. The Hebrew preposition *k* sometimes has the force of "as something **in**" (see P. Joüon & T. Muraoka, *Grammar of Biblical Hebrew*.
2. Luther's *Werke* (Weimar, 1883), vol. 5, p. 608.

IV. Seeking the Power

The Baptism with the Spirit: A Question of Method

The theology of the baptism with the Spirit is the crucial dividing line between "charismatic" and "non-charismatic" (in the way those terms are often used). Can anything new be said? Yes, I think there is still room for continued discussion and clarification of the questions involved. After forty years or so of discussion it has surely become clear that different people come to different conclusions about the gift of the Spirit because of different methods of establishing doctrine from Scripture. **The crucial question is whether the gift of the Spirit is experiential or is rather a sub-conscious event**.

I call my little exposition "a charismatic approach". It might well be asked, "Is there a specially 'charismatic approach' to preaching which is different from the approach of someone who is less 'pentecostal'?" I believe there is. The difference between the charismatic and non-charismatic approach to preaching is parallel to the difference between the charismatic and non-charismatic approach to the baptism with the Spirit. Non-charismatics (forgive the horribly negative term!) generally regard the baptism with the Spirit as non-experiential. Pentecostals generally and "Calvinistic Pentecostals" like myself in particular regard the baptism with the Spirit as a distinct and definite experience. I think in this connection of something that Dr J.I. Packer said to me when I asked him a question back in the late 1960s. He was speaking at an IVF (now UCCF) conference at Swanick (a conference centre) in Britain. At one point I went to ask him a question. I began to ask the question: "Your argument that the gift of the Holy Spirit is an initial experience..." Packer interrupted me. "I did not say that!" "Oh," I said, rather puzzled, "but I thought..." Packer was swift to explain. "I did not say that the gift of the Holy Spirit is an initial **experience**; I said that the gift of the Holy Spirit is an initial **event**..." Packer's words to me at that time put the non-Pentecostal view perfectly. The baptism with the Spirit is an **event**, but it is not an **experience**. It is below the level of consciousness.

I believe evangelical non-charismatic thinking has gone astray here. Conservative Christians and "reformed" Christians (I am one of them but I seem to be able to combine my "Reformed" theology with some Pentecostal strands of thinking) tend to play down experience. John Piper writes a chapter about the power of the Holy Spirit in preaching. There is nothing in it that I disagree with. Yet there is something missing, in my opinion. Half of the chapter about the power of the Spirit is taken up with insisting that the Spirit is the revealer of the Word. Well that is true enough – but it means that a chapter on the Spirit is taken up by being a half-chapter on the Word! On the Day of Pentecost the Word of God was certainly there but everyone was very conscious of the **felt** and even **visible** working of the Holy Spirit. A lot of the teaching in certain sections of evangelicalism seems to focus on what I could call the **secret** work of the Spirit. This was Calvin's strong point. He was a "theologian of the Holy Spirit" as B.B. Warfield said. But we ought to notice how Calvin focused on the hidden and secret work of the Spirit. This is fine by me. There is indeed a secret work of the Spirit. Regeneration is a hidden work.

It was not a **mistake** but an **omission** on the part of Calvin when he said very little about **experiences** of the Spirit. And it is this that I find missing in so many "conservative" or "Reformed" expositions of the power of the Spirit. In the New Testament everything is vibrantly experiential. "You shall receive power..." said Jesus. Is there such a thing as non-experiential power? Is there non-experiential "joy unspeakable"? If the Holy Spirit is a down-payment of the joys and experiences of heaven, is it to be experience-less?

Let me argue again for the charismatic viewpoint. The starting point is surely this. We must be more aware than seems to be the case that **numerous interchangeable terms are used in Scripture to refer to what is often called the baptism with the Spirit**. The actual phrase "to baptize with the Spirit" comes certainly six times in the New Testament (Matthew 3:11; Mark 1:8; Luke 3:16; John 1:33; Acts 1:5; 11:16) and possibly (if 1 Corinthians 12:13 is included) seven times. Reading the New Testament it soon becomes evident that this phrasing is by no means the only one that is used and that a number of other terms are used to describe the same spiritual blessing. The matter of interchangeable terminology is stressed by almost anyone who wishes to stress the experience of the Spirit.[1] It is the larger sweep of New Testament Scriptures that makes it clear that the baptism with the Spirit is something experiential. Writers who wish to down-play the experience of the Spirit often cling to 1 Corinthians 12:13, as if that verse alone were the source of understanding of the baptism with the Spirit. The evidence of interchangeability is worth our consideration.

Consider Acts chapters 1 and 2. In Acts 1:4 Jesus refers to the "promise of the Father" and immediately goes on to describe the promise as a matter of being "baptized with the Spirit" (1:5). Three verses later – and there is no reason to think there is any change of subject – Jesus speaks of the Spirit's "coming upon" the disciples and of their "receiving power" (Acts 1:8). The four terms all refer to what is about to happen. The next chapter of Acts describes the long-awaited event, but now several other terms are introduced. The event is perhaps called "being filled" in Acts 2:4 (although one remembers Lloyd-Jones's view that at this point two things are happening at the same time). The same Pentecostal event is the Spirit's being "poured forth" or "poured out" or "shed abroad" according to Acts 2:18, 33. It is identified with a term that has already been used – "promise of the Father" – in Acts 2:33. When at the time of Peter's sermon an offer is made to the

responsive crowd – "you shall receive the gift of the Holy Spirit" –
there is no reason to think anything different is being referred to. So
we are given the impression that the Spirit's being "given" and the
phrase "you shall receive" still indicate the same spiritual blessing.

All of this means that within two chapters of Acts eight
expressions are used all of which refer to the same spiritual blessing.
I do not suggest these terms are all *precisely* synonymous, yet they
do all refer to the same blessing.

Consider next Acts chapters 10 and 11. We read of some gentile
people who received the Spirit. As Cornelius and his friends listened
to Peter, the Spirit "fell on" them (10:44). To describe the same
event the verb "poured out" is also used (10:45). Another phrase
tells us that they "received" the Spirit. When Peter tells the story he
uses again the term "fell on" and identifies what had happened with
what happened on the day of Pentecost ("even as on us at the
beginning", 11:15). Further on in the narrative he uses the term
"baptized with the Spirit" (11:16). Most of these terms have already
been used in connection with the day of Pentecost but there is a
new term introduced ("fell upon"), which makes a total of nine
terms that are used of the same spiritual experience.

Consider next what happened to Jesus in the river Jordan.
In Luke 3:22 this event is called "receiving power". We may compare
Luke 3:22 with Luke 4:14 and 4:18, and then note the similarity of
phrasing with the phrases used by the same author in Luke 24:49 and
Acts 1:8. Clearly what happened to Jesus is comparable to what
happened to the disciples on the day of Pentecost, and, therefore, the
same terminology may be used. Yet one term for this same spiritual
experience is "anointing" (see Luke 4:18; Acts 10:38). Can we believe
this is anything different? I think not.

We now have ten terms in Luke-Acts which are provably
interchangeable:

- the promise of the Father
- being baptized with the Spirit
- the Spirit's coming upon people

- receiving power
- being filled with the Spirit
- the Spirit's being poured out
- the gift of the Spirit
- the Spirit's being received
- the Spirit's falling on people
- the anointing of the Spirit.

Now let us move from Luke to Paul. In Ephesians 1:13–14 the Ephesians were described as being "sealed with the Spirit". The fact that Paul adds "of the promise" immediately reminds us of the "promise of the Father" that we have already been considering. Clearly the "sealing" is identical with "the promise of the Father" which was given on the day of Pentecost (yet Paul is writing Ephesians decades after the day of Pentecost and the "Ephesians" to whom the letter is sent include gentiles who cannot have been present on the day of Pentecost). When Paul goes on to say that this "sealing" is to be identified with "the down-payment of our inheritance"; he is quite explicitly identifying the sealing of the Spirit with the "earnest" or "down-payment" of the Spirit.

Then in 2 Corinthians 1:21–22, Paul uses not two terms (as in Ephesians 1:13–14) but three! Paul refer to God's work of "establishing" the believer; God has "anointed us . . . sealed us . . . and has given the down-payment of the Spirit." Are these not three aspects of the one gift of the Spirit? Surely we must agree with the English Puritan Richard Sibbes. Three metaphors ("three borrowed terms" said Sibbes) are used but they all refer to the same spiritual reality.[2] Again we have interchangeable terms.

It is surely clear that we have here a whole network of terms which are provably interchangeable. Ten terms are interchangeable (in the sense of being used to refer to the same reality) in Luke-Acts. These terms overlap with another network of four terms used by Paul.

- sealed with the Spirit
- promise of the Father

- the down-payment of our inheritance
- God "anointed us"

Two terms, "promise of the Father", "anointed" occur in both lists. Not only are the terms interchangeable within each group; the entire groups are interchangeable. There are now twelve terms which all may be used in connection with the baptism with the Holy Spirit. All of these terms are demonstrably interchangeable. What about the other terms that Lloyd-Jones uses: Spirit of adoption, the Spirit's crying "Abba Father", the witness of the Spirit? What of the firstfruits of the Spirit in Romans 8:23? What of the references to the Spirit in John 7:37–39 and John 14–16?

There is good reason to think that most of these must be included in the list of interchangeable terms also. Consideration of the **content** of each phrase suggests that many of these refer to the same spiritual reality, commonly in recent decades called the "baptism with the Spirit". Is there any conceptual difference between the "down-payment" and the "firstfruits" of the Spirit? Do they not both refer to the fact that the Spirit gives a touch of the glories of heaven, a taste of the world of the resurrection (see 2 Corinthians 5:5 which comes in a passage referring to final resurrection)? If they are similar in **content** we must include them in the list of interchangeable terms. In Galatians 4:6–7 reference is made to the Spirit's giving us a sense of sonship. Surely this would be a "seal" to us of our salvation, and a foretaste of the fellowship of heaven? Paul's point in Galatians 3:1–5 is that the gift of the Spirit sealed the Galatians' salvation – their justification only by the hearing of faith. The situation in Galatians was comparable to the situation in Acts chapters 10–11.

We have to say that constant study of this wide range of terms constantly reveals interconnections of thought and of content, and constantly reinforces the conviction that these many terms all fall under the heading of **one** concept.

The Johannine vocabulary has distinctives of its own. It lacks some of the terms used by Luke and Paul and must be considered on its own without too hasty an integration with the Lucan and Pauline terminology. Yet it seems clear (and I do not think many Bible-believing Christians would doubt it) that the Paraclete promises of John 14–16 refer to what John had earlier called the "baptism with the Spirit" in John 1:33. John 14–16 refers to some kind of receiving of the Spirit at an **experiential** level. John has other expressions (notably "new birth") for designating something else.

These brief remarks must suffice for the moment as just a hint of what is needed: a thorough survey of the terminology of the New Testament vocabulary concerning the Holy Spirit. Others, such as M.B. Turner,[3] have already done something similar and at fuller length. Such studies invariably come to the same conclusion: a large number of biblical expressions refer to the same reality that is commonly called the baptism with the Spirit. The Puritans, Richard Sibbes and Thomas Goodwin saw it a long time ago. Lloyd-Jones assumed it without much discussion. It must be specially noted, since it is the starting-point of any investigation into the nature of the baptism with the Spirit. Writers who cling to 1 Corinthians 12:13 alone will accidentally twist the biblical evidence.

The matter of interchangeable terms is important since to miss this observation will affect the exposition of the New Testament accounts of the work of the Spirit. The comments made by Stibbs and Packer on Acts 8 serve to illustrate this very point. They argue that:

> "... the Samaritan converts spoken of in Acts 8 ... were persons whom Christ had undoubtedly baptized with the Spirit. Their subsequent 'receiving' of the Holy Spirit (verses 15, 17, 19) would appear to have had to do only with the special manifestations ... Note that in Acts 8:16 the record says that the Spirit 'had not yet fallen on any of them'. The point of this phraseology apparently is ... that no one had experienced any accompanying manifestations."[4]

However to read through Acts 10 and 11 is to discover immediately that "to baptize with the Spirit", to "receive the Spirit" and to have the Spirit "fall on" believers are equivalent expressions (see Acts

10:44 and 11:15–17). To introduce a distinction between the Spirit's "falling on" believers and their being "baptized" with the Spirit is to neglect Luke's terminological usage and to fail to note the interchangeability of terms. Interestingly, considering the views of Packer and Stibbs, we note also their admission that "receive" is used of a post-regeneration "experience" of the Spirit!

We have to accept the fact that there is good reason for maintaining the essential identity of a large range of New Testament Scriptures as source material for a study of the baptism with the Spirit. A full doctrine of the baptism with the Spirit must not confine itself to the six or (some would say) seven references where that terminology is used (in verbal form). The major scriptures that must be contextually studied in elucidating a biblical view of the baptism with the Spirit are:

> Isaiah 32:15; 44:3–5; Ezekiel 39:29; Joel 2:28–29; Matthew 3:11, 16; Mark 1:8; Luke 3:16; 4:14, 18; 24:49; John 1:33; 7:37–39; 14–16; Acts chapters 1, 2, 8, 10, 11, 19; Romans 5:5; 8:15, 23; 2 Corinthians 1:21–22; 5:5; Galatians 3:2, 14; Ephesians 1:13–14; 4:30; Titus 3:6.

When we ask our questions, it is from these Scriptures (at least initially) that we get our answers.

I have left out Romans 8:16 from this survey! I do so since the Greek verb in Romans 8:16 has a present tense. It does not refer to a striking single event in precisely the same way as the other terms we have considered. Lloyd-Jones's view was that Romans 8:16 focuses in detail on what happens as the event of the baptism with the Spirit is taking place, and that it goes beyond Romans 8:15. I recall (but cannot document) times when he accidentally and instinctively added the word "also" ("The Spirit *also* witnesses with our spirits . . . "). This is what Paul **ought** to have said if Lloyd-Jones's view of the relationship between Romans 8:15 and 8:16 was totally accurate – but of course Paul did not say "also"! I have a different view of the precise relationship of Romans 8:15 to 8:16. I need not go into it here.[5] Romans 8:16 certainly seems to belong to the same circle of ideas as "sealing", "foretaste" and the other terms, and yet it refers to something more continuous and less "aoristic". We need not include it in our list of terms referring to an "aoristic" (decisive, taking place on a definite occasion) event.

I have left out 1 Corinthians 12:13 for reasons I state fully elsewhere.[6] Certainly a doctrine cannot be derived from 1 Corinthians 12:13 alone. Judged by the main scriptural passages that deal with the subject, the baptism with the Spirit is undoubtedly an experiential event. If the *entire* range of biblical material is surveyed, the irresistible conclusion is reached that the baptism with the Spirit is an **experiential** gift. In Old Testament prediction, the "outpouring" of the Spirit is portrayed in experiential terms. It is the end of being thirsty; it is a gift of assurance in which one calls oneself by the name of Jacob and writes on one's hands "belonging to the Lord" (Isaiah 32:15; 44:3–5). It is the end of God's hiding His face (Ezekiel 39:29); that is to say, it is the coming in of a new and richer consciousness of God's presence. It is the occasion when God's people **experience** prophetic endowment (Joel 2:28–29).

Similarly, the New Testament descriptions are irritably experiential. Can one experience "rivers of living water" non-experientially (John 7:37–39)? When the love of God is "poured out" or "shed abroad" in (not **into**) one's heart, surely this refers to a **consciousness** of God's love towards us (Romans 5:5)? To receive the "Spirit of adoption in whom one cries, 'Abba Father' " (Romans 8:15) is surely experiential. How can one "cry Abba father" non-experientially? In 2 Corinthians 1:21–22 the surrounding context speaks of one's being "established" and of Paul's not vacillating because he has received the anointing-seal-down-payment of the Spirit. Can something entirely non-experiential have a stabilizing effect on one's life? Surely a "down-payment" of final glory has to be experiential? Heaven is a place of fellowship, love, worship, consciousness of the presence of God. If one has a part-payment of the rewards of heaven, a little bit of heaven to go to heaven in, it has to include experiential blessings. It surely means that we experience a little of the worship, praise, joy and love of heaven **now**. Can this be non-experiential? In 2 Corinthians 5:5 the gift of the Spirit is a foretaste of the rewards that come with the resurrection body. If the foretaste is non-experiential, how can it be a foretaste?

In Galatians 3:1–5 Paul looks back on a **memorable** event, connected with the coming of miracles. He uses the occasion of the gift of the Spirit upon the Galatians to prove to them his doctrine of justification by faith. But how can he use the receiving of the Spirit to prove justification by faith if the receiving of the Spirit is not an experienced and remembered event? Surely Galatians 3:1–5 alludes to something analogous or identical to Acts 10 where a "receiving of the Spirit" put a complete end to the question as to whether Gentiles could or could not experience salvation. Some writers do not seem to notice that Galatians 3:1–5 is an appeal to experience. When an evangelical writer speaks of "the initial entrance of the Holy Spirit into the hearts when they [the converts] put their trust in the Lord Jesus", he is in effect giving a non-experiential understanding of the passage. He does not explain **how** they know the Spirit came upon them. The passage makes no sense if the converts' gift of the Spirit is "taken by faith" in the same way justification is "taken by faith". Paul is appealing to **experience** to prove justification which is non-experiential.[7] He uses something experiential to prove something non-experiential. Thomas Aquinas was closer to Paul's argument, surely, in seeing allusion to "**manifest** signs of the Holy Spirit" which "took place in the hearers immediately after the apostles preached the faith." They "**openly** received the Holy Spirit at Paul's preaching," he says. Aquinas is identifying the receiving of the Spirit in Galatians 3:1–5 with the receiving of the charismata. This may not be the whole story but at least it does focus attention on the nature of Paul's appeal to experience.[8] Paul's appeal to conscious experience is of the essence of his argument. The "blessing of Abraham", the gift of the Spirit (Galatians 3:14) is experiential according to Galatians 3:1–5.

In Ephesians 1:13–14 the "sealing" is identified with a foretaste of final redemption. This too must mean that final glory is partially **experienced** in the here-and-now. Ephesians 4:30 asks us to live in such a way that the **experienced** sealing of the Spirit is not damaged.

In the book of Acts the various outpourings of the Spirit in Acts chapters 1, 2, 8, 10, 11, 19, are surely all vibrantly experiential. We remember Lloyd-Jones's comment: "Not experiential! Nothing can be more experiential; it is the height of Christian experience."

Notes

1. It was stressed in the early days of the Charismatic movement by such writers as Michael Harper (see *Power for the Body of Christ* (London: Fountain Trust, 1964), p. 10).
2. J. Piper, *The Supremacy of God in Preaching* (Kingsway, 1990), pp. 37–46.
3. See his earlier articles "Spirit-Endowment in Luke-Acts: Some Linguistic Considerations", *Vox Evangelica*, 12 (1981), pp. 45–63; "Jesus and the Spirit in Lucan Perspective", *Tyndale Bulletin*, 32 (1981), pp. 3–42; "The Significance of Spirit Endowment for Paul", *Vox Evangelica*, 9 (1975), pp. 56–69; "The Concept of Receiving the Spirit in John's Gospel", *Vox Evangelica*, 10 (1977), pp. 24–42.
4. See A.M. Stibbs and J.I. Packer, *The Spirit Within You* (London: Hodder and Stoughton, 1967), p. 35.
5. I go into the matter in M.A. Eaton, *Everlasting Security* (Sermons on Romans 8) – which awaits publication.
6. See M.A. Eaton, *1 Corinthians 10–16* (PTTB, Sovereign World).
7. See K.S. Wuest, *Galatians in the Greek New Testament* (Grand Rapids: Eerdmans, n.d.), p. 85; see also H.D. MacDonald, *Freedom in Faith: A Commentary on . . . Galatians* (London: Pickering and Inglis, 1973), p. 6.
8. *Thomas Aquinas, Commentary on Saint Paul's Epistle to the Galatians* Aquinas Scripture Series, vol. 1 (Albany USA: Magi, 1966), p. 71. The bold text is mine. Fuller emphasis on the experiential aspect of the gift of the Spirit is found in C.P. Cousar, *Galatians – Interpretation* (Atlanta: John Knox, 1982), esp. p. 69. A. Viard also links the gift of the Spirit mentioned here with the Spirit's bestowal in Acts 10:44 and draws attention to the Spirit's effusion with exterior manifestations (*Saint Paul, Épître aux Galates, Sources Bibliques*, Paris: Gabalda, 1964), p. 62.

The Experience of the Spirit

It is constant outpourings of the Holy Spirit which are needed if anyone is to exercise any spiritual power. No one could have been present on any of these New Testament occasions when the Spirit was poured out without an there being a sharp **awareness** of the spiritual events taking place. In short, the experiential nature of the gift of the Spirit can only be denied if attention is focused exclusively on 1 Corinthians 12:13 and the wider evidence is ignored or disparaged.

It is interesting to notice a number of writers who deny any idea of an outpouring of the Spirit distinct from conversion, who are nevertheless sensitive to this point. James Dunn is widely regarded as a writer who refutes Pentecostalism. Anti-charismatic preachers recommend his work[1] as a kind of refutation of the Charismatic movement. But they have not always paid attention to what James Dunn actually says! He is not an evangelical and is strongly critical of the evangelical view of Scripture. Closer attention to his work would reveal that he is more pentecostal than the Pentecostals! Far from denying the experiential nature of the gift of the Spirit he asserts it very strongly. However, Dunn views the "Pentecostal" experience as itself Christian conversion. Unless one has had a Pentecostal-type experience one is not a Christian at all, judged by New Testament standards. For Dunn an **experiential** baptism with the Spirit is the chief element in conversion-initiation (Dunn's phrase for the whole complex of elements in conversion, including water-baptism). He goes on to say it was a very definite and often dramatic **experience**; the Pentecostal's belief in the dynamic and experiential nature of Spirit baptism is, for James Dunn, well founded. Although in Dunn's view the Pentecostal's **separation** of Spirit baptism from conversion is objectionable, the nature of it as a "Pentecostal" **experience** is not. Dunn's work may argue against a post-conversion experiential gift of the Spirit, but every page of his work bears witness to the experiential nature of the gift. It is only the idea of its being "post-conversion" that he opposes. Whether he is right to say one is not a Christian without this experience is a matter for further discussion, but his evidence that the gift is experiential cannot be easily resisted. In James Dunn, opponents of charismatic teaching have caught a tiger by the tail. It is only by receiving the Spirit (interpreted in a strongly Pentecostal fashion) that one becomes a Christian, according to Dunn's interpretation of the Lucan writings.[2] He says, "That the Spirit and particularly the gift of the Spirit was a **fact of experience** in the lives of the earliest Christians has been too obvious to require elaboration."[3] He is exactly right. We have to follow one of three theological directions here. (i) Either **only** those who have had Pentecostal experience may be called Christians, or (ii) such experience is **not** the *sine qua non* of being a Christian (and it is therefore "subsequent" to Christian conversion if experienced at all. Or (iii) we accept that the New Testament presents one picture of a Christian but (on one ground or another) we justify an altogether different picture and treat the New Testament as without authority. The latter option will raise questions as to our doctrine of Scripture, and whether the New Testament is normative in its description of what a Christian is. It is possible for a theologian to accept the third route (and so follow a non-evangelical doctrine of Scripture). But if this is done the disregard of Scripture ought to be openly acknowledged. Personally, I adopt the second route and believe that **subsequent** to Christian conversion one's experience may catch up with what one possesses objectively and in principle from conversion onwards. The term baptism with the Spirit ought, in my judgement, to be used not of what is in principle given from conversion onwards, but of what is known in experience, which may or may not take place at the time of coming to faith in Christ.

Another writer who accepts that this experiential note is to be found in the New Testament descriptions of the gift of the Spirit is the Roman Catholic, Francis A. Sullivan. Sullivan points to the "experiential aspect of New Testament 'baptism in the Spirit'."[4] He wishes to argue that two aspects are involved in the baptism with the Spirit, what he calls the theological and the experiential. I am happy with this but wish to ask whether there would be any essential difference in theology if baptism in the Spirit is used in the New Testament **only** of the experiential half? What if everything that there is to have by way of Christian blessing is given **objectively and in principle** at Christian conversion but that the New Testament name for coming to an experiential realization of sonship is called "baptism with the Spirit"?

The baptism with the Spirit is associated in the New Testament with assurance, power, prayer, joy, emotion in prayer (or is crying Abba Father non-experiential?), assurance concerning future glory and the resurrection body. It is all vibrantly experiential. There is no question of our having to "take it by faith" that we have received the Spirit. There are about fifty or so references to the outpouring of the Spirit (of course there are hundreds, but I mean fifty or so that **focus** on the subject). It is a mistake to look at them all through 1 Corinthians 12:13 (which is indeed something non-experiential, and that is the proof that 1 Corinthians 12:13 is distinct from the vibrantly experiential outpourings and baptisms found all over the New Testament). Our union with Christ has to be "reckoned" but no one needed to "reckon" anything on the day of Pentecost! Experiences do not need to be reckoned; sub-conscious events do. This is itself the proof that 1 Corinthians 12:13 and what is generally called the baptism with the Spirit – are distinct.

Is the baptism with the identical to regeneration? No. Old Testament saints were regenerate (in the sense of being brought to faith by the quickening of the spirit). The apostles were regenerate before Pentecost. If it be said that only in **their** case were the two distinct and **now** they come together – I reply, "It only takes one person ever in the history of the world to be regenerate first and baptised with the Spirit second to prove they are distinct!" Was Jesus being born again in the river Jordan? No. Were the disciples getting born again – again – on the Day of Pentecost? No! However unusual and unique their experience might have been it is quite clear that regeneration and the outpouring of the Spirit were distinct.

I cannot argue these matters out in detail here. Space forbids. But here is surely the secret of power in preaching – the baptism with the Spirit! We are surely to expect and pray for and **experience** powerful leadings and experiences of the Spirit in our preaching. A secret work of the Spirit is fine, but the New Testament leads us to expect to be also **conscious** of the Holy Spirit – and for everyone else around us to be conscious of the Spirit as well. Consider 1 Thessalonians 1:5. Paul says, *"We know . . . that you have been chosen* (1:4), *because our gospel did not come to you in word only but it came to you in power and in the Holy Spirit and with much conviction"* (1:5). The heart and centre of what happened in the spiritual awakening at Thessalonica was a combination of the Word of God and the Holy Spirit. The balance between "Word and Spirit" is well known, although it does not answer all questions (since most people think they are "balanced"!) In our preaching there has to be "word"; there must be substance. Christian ministry is proclamation, a clear announcement of what God is doing. There is a telling-out of good news in a comprehensible manner. In the gospels Jesus would teach publicly in the synagogues, in the temple courts, or in the open air. There must be word. Our God has plenty to say.

Yet the power of the Holy Spirit must also be present. How does this "power of the Holy Spirit" show itself? It is not just a matter of "phenomena". Sometimes, when preaching is in the power of the Holy Spirit, there are unusual phenomena. There may be unusual effects on people's bodies. But this is not the main thing, and the apostles did not deliberately seek phenomena although unusual events often took place as they preached.

This power of the Holy Spirit brings liberty of speech. He gives clarity of understanding, authority, fearlessness. Think of Peter's preaching on the day of Pentecost. A few weeks before he had been muddled and confused, and had avoided being involved with Jesus at the time of Jesus' arrest. When the Spirit came upon him, he immediately was given what to say and said it with great liberty, fearlessness and with deep understanding of what had happened in the death and resurrection of Jesus. Within seconds he had received a profound grasp of what had just happened on the Day of Pentecost.

This power of the Holy Spirit brings "much assurance". The preacher has assurance about what he is preaching. The people have deep conviction that what they are hearing is from God.

All of this is powerfully experiential! How can anyone reading the New Testament play down **experience** of God? What is the Book of Acts if it is not a sample of what happens when God is powerfully at work? Must we get rid of it and say, "It was only for those days. Don't try to learn too much from the Book of Acts"?

Have you ever noticed how Acts 4 follows Acts chapter 2 and there is a fresh enduement with power? This is a couple of days after Pentecost. Suddenly there is this crisis and people are arrested. The Church starts praying; they say, "Lord, give us boldness." They do not say, "Please, Lord, don't let us get arrested." They do not say, "Don't let us be persecuted." They do not say, "We're sorry, Lord, we disturbed the peace a bit, we promise we won't do it again." They said, 'Please, Lord, give us more boldness." And the place is shaken, the very building shakes, like an earthquake. And they are **filled with the Holy Spirit**. It's the same people who were filled with the Holy Spirit a couple of days before. They are filled **again!** There's a fresh outpouring of the Holy Spirit. And they go out and they do the very thing they've just been told not to do – they preach the gospel with boldness. We need this baptism with power. And we don't just need it on one occasion in our life, we need repetitions and renewals. We need God to anoint us and touch us and come with us and be there with His presence, day by day.

A lot of books on expository preaching seem to be **actually** books on expository lecturing. What makes preaching to be preaching is the power of the Holy Spirit. When it comes to the power of the Holy Spirit there seems to be a "take it by faith" atmosphere about some of these expository preachers. We are meant to take it by faith that the Spirit is doing a hidden work of conviction. That is certainly a biblical idea. Often God brings us to new levels in relationship with Him without our being conscious that God is at work as we are making new discoveries. The work of the Spirit may well be hidden from us. But is this all there is to the power of the Spirit? The expository preachers seem to often to put the emphasis on the first word, not the second. They talk about teaching technique and persuading congregations to get used to their style of expository lecturing. But just as I fear that the Charismatic movement has been an experience without a theology, it would be just as bad to have a theology – even a theology of expository preaching – without an experience! We like to talk about the balance between Word and Spirit. That is fine. But how do we know what the balance is? How many people think they are unbalanced? We can all find extremists to the left of us and to the right of us, so we can all claim to be balanced!

The balance is in the Book of Acts. The Bible is a balanced book. The book of Acts is not extremist, it is normal New Testament Christianity. If we are a long way from the Book of Acts (and we all are!) then it is we who are the unbalanced ones, not the New Testament!

We need the experiences of the Spirit that were experienced in the Book of Acts. We must continually remember that the Book of Acts is the book of the Bible that more than any other defines what the Church is. The story starts with an outpouring of the Spirit. God had promised that this would happen to His people, both in the Old Testament, and through the words of Jesus. So they prayed for this promise to be fulfilled. They could not take it by faith; God had to give this gift of the Holy Spirit. People who try to "take" the baptism of the Spirit are normally no different and their preaching is more lecturing than preaching! God has to **give** the Spirit, no one can "take it" or switch on the gift of the Spirit at will. In Acts chapter 4 the gift of the Spirit leads to great fellowship and warmth among the Christians in the newly enlarged church in Jerusalem. Then there are signs and wonders and Peter uses these signs and wonders as the starting-point of his preaching. He does not say much about the miracles themselves, he simply uses them to point to Jesus. Acts 3–4 tells the story of one of these incidents. A miracle takes place. Peter starts preaching. He and his colleague are arrested, but they are not afraid. How is it that these fishermen without any special academic training are able to speak so clearly and boldly and convincingly? Their enemies know the answer! These men have been with Jesus! They have been disciples of the man they crucified about eight weeks before. There is powerful evidence in the lives of Peter and John that what the Jewish authorities are confronting is real.

The Jewish leaders use threats and intimidation. They want to suppress this preaching altogether. They command them not to do any more preaching. But the apostles are fearless, unapologetic, and with regard to their message they are unyielding. They ask a question: "You judge for yourselves," says Peter "and tell us what you would do if you were in our place." It is a very bold and piercing way of getting the parliamentarians to think about what they were doing. "If you knew that Jesus was raised from the dead and had healed this man – you tell us! – what would you do?"

The apostles are very daring. What if they should be killed? But how can people who have just witnessed the resurrection of Jesus have any fear of death? Jesus was killed only eight weeks before and look at what happened! Why should they or we fear death – or anything or anyone?

But **the leaders of Israel respond with a second rejection of the gospel**. Peter is speaking to the leaders of the entire nation. He has been constantly emphasizing this very point. The miracle took place at the temple – the supreme centre of Israel's faith. Peter had addressed the people as "people of Israel". The capital city was getting a chance to change its mind. If they will see that Jesus' death is part of God's plan, if they will receive Him as Saviour, there will be refreshing times for the whole nation (3:20). It is the national parliament who are interrogating these apostles just as they interrogated Jesus eight weeks before. The high-priestly family are there, just as they had been present at Jesus' trial. Here is the entire nation of Jesus being given a second chance. Once again they may receive or reject Jesus at a national level.

But now the Spirit has been poured out. A largish minority of people in Jerusalem have come to faith. Everyone knows about this healing and they are praising God for what has happened. What did the apostles do when they found themselves in danger of persecution? They prayed! They went to their new friends, the thousands who had come to faith in Christ, and they told them what had happened (4:23). Then they all prayed. It was **loud** praying. They "lifted up their voice" (4:24). It was **united** praying. They are all speaking at the same time. The words of their prayer (4:24b–30) records a summary of what their praying all amounted to. It was **Bible-based** praying. They took a psalm of the Old Testament and made it the foundation of their praying. They have only one request. The ask for boldness and for God's help in giving signs and wonders. They do not pray for an easier time. They do not apologize to God for bringing trouble upon themselves ("Please forgive us for causing so much disturbance.") Not at all! The do not even pray for the conversion of their enemies. They hand their enemies over to God (4:29a). They pray to be given boldness in spreading God's word (4:29b). And they ask that God will give supporting signs and wonders as they do so (4:30).

Consider the result of their praying. We are seeing what all this must mean to us. This is what the Church is! The Church is not some cosy group of religious people hiding in holy buildings. *"And when they had prayed, the place in which they were gathered together was shaken; and they were all filled with the Holy Spirit and spoke the word of*

God with boldness" (4:31). They received a further outpouring of the power of the Holy Spirit.

Can the Day of Pentecost be repeated? Can we receive baptisms with the Spirit again and again? I think the answer is yes (though the word "baptism" is used for the first time we **consciously** receive the power of the Spirit!) Consider Acts 4:31 and compare it with Acts 2. On the day of Pentecost there were miraculous phenomena (the wind, the fire); in Acts 4 there was a miraculous phenomenon (the shaking building). In Acts 2 they were praying and God blessed them while they prayed. Something similar happened in Acts 4. In Acts they were given power to become bold witnesses (Acts 1:8). In Acts 4 they prayed for and received great boldness (4:31). In Acts 2 they were "filled" with the Spirit (2:4). In Acts 4 they were "filled" with the Spirit (4:31). Can the Day of Pentecost be repeated? Well, almost everything that happened in Acts 2 happened again in Acts 4! The Day of Pentecost was an outpouring of spiritual power upon a Church that was already in existence. We use the term "baptized with the Spirit" for the **first** outpouring of the Spirit. But there can be fresh outpourings of the Spirit again and again. In such cases we use the term "filled". We may not experience shaken buildings every day, but the Church is the place where Jesus acts in power. Through His people His plans for the world go forward. Outpourings of the Holy Spirit are the way in which the Church makes progress.

I close with one of my favourite stories which has influenced me all my life. I read it as a teenager. It deeply challenged me then, and I have been influenced by it ever since. There was an old preacher once. He was getting ready to preach and was in the vestry (the room at the back of the church). The congregation was out there in the auditorium, ready to hear his preaching. But he was still getting ready and was staying there a long time in the vestry. The time to preach had come and he still had not come out of the vestry. So they sent a servant girl (this is in the nineteenth century) to go and get him. So she goes to tell him it is time to preach, and she comes back and she says, "I didn't interrupt him, he was busy talking to somebody." And they said, "Alright, we'll give him a bit longer." And then another five minutes went by and they sent her back again: "Go and tell him we're ready waiting for him." She goes and she comes back and she's still not got him. She says, "No, he's talking to somebody. I know he's talking to somebody because I heard what he said. I heard him say, 'I will not go out in front of those people unless **you** come with me.'" Of course, he was talking to God. He was praying. "I will not go out, I will not leave this room and talk to those people unless I **know** that you are coming with me." Do you remember Moses? "Lord, if your presence go not with us, carry us not up hence." The preacher would not walk out of his vestry unless he had assurance that **God** would be coming out with him. And although you may know something of the baptism of the Holy Spirit, you need to be baptised with the Holy Spirit every time you preach. You need a fresh power from God; the old power will not do.

We need to prepare (in every sense!) for powerful – prophetic – expository – preaching. I stress every word. Our prophetic preachers need to be more scholarly. The scholars have let us down; we and our friends shall have to do the work ourselves. We need to **believe** in the prophetic. We are not university lecturers – though some of us could do that easily enough! Little young Jeremiah was scared to be a prophet. God had an answer for him. *"Then the LORD put out his hand and touched my mouth. And the LORD said to me, Behold, I have put my words in your mouth."* God can still do it, and when He does the revival we are waiting for will be upon us.

Notes

1. Notably *Baptism in the Holy Spirit* (SCM, 1970). His *Jesus and the Spirit* (SCM, 1975) is also important.
2. See J. Dunn, *Baptism in the Holy Spirit* (London: SCM, 1970), p. 4.
3. Dunn, *Baptism*, p. 225.
4. F.A. Sullivan, *Charisms and Charismatic Renewal* (Dublin: Gill and Macmillan, 1982), pp. 66–70.

We hope you enjoyed reading this New Wine book.
For details of other New Wine books
and a wide range of titles from other
Word and Spirit publishers visit our website:
www.newwineministries.co.uk
email: newwine@xalt.co.uk